A MANUAL OF
WRITER'S TRICKS

Also Available From Marlowe & Company

Ghostwriting by Eva Shaw

How To Make A Living As A Travel Writer by Susan Farewell

How To Prepare Your Manuscript by David L. Carroll

How To Write Science Fiction by Matthew J. Costello

A Manual of Writer's Tricks by David L. Carroll

Trade Secrets by Eva Shaw

The Use and Abuse of the English Language
by Robert Graves and Alan Hodge

Writing and Selling Magazine Articles by Eva Shaw

Writing Effective Speeches by Henry Enrlich

Writing True-Life Stories by Susan C. Feldhake

A
MANUAL
OF
WRITER'S
TRICKS

David L. Carroll

MARLOWE & COMPANY
New York

Second edition, 1995

Published in the United States by

Marlowe & Company
632 Broadway, Seventh Floor
New York, N.Y. 10012

Designed by Eve Kirch

Library of Congress Cataloging-in-Publication Data

Carroll, David, 1942–
    A manual of writer's tricks / by David L. Carroll. — 1st ed.
       p.   cm.
    ISBN 1-56924-877-X
    1. Authorship.   2. Style, Literary.   I. Title.
PN145.C325   1990
808'.02—dc20   89-26586
                                                                     CIP

Manufactured in the United States of America

The paper used in this publication meets the minimum requirements of
American National Standard for Information Sciences—Permanence of
Paper for Printed Library Materials, ANSI Z39.48-1984.

Contents

Contents

Introduction

WHY HENRY'S FACE WAS RED

MANY years ago I read a Helen Hokinson cartoon in *The New Yorker* that has stayed bemusedly fixed in my memory ever since. It shows two pudgy matrons standing in an upper-middle class parlor. One of them calls to her beleagured looking husband in the next room, saying proudly and not without a touch of boastfulness, "Henry, *do* show Priscilla that nice rejection letter you got from *The Atlantic Monthly*."

"Nice" rejection letter. It's a contradiction in terms, really, a kind of oxymoron, sort of like saying "friendly fire" or "painless dentistry." Henry's face is appropriately red.

Why is his face red? Because a writer's *raison d'être* is to be accepted, not rejected, whether by *The Atlantic Monthly*, the professor who oversees our course, or a major publisher. We write to be recognized—and anything we can do to further this aim is welcome.

There are, of course, two areas in any written document that cause it to succeed or fail: Content (what we say) and style (the way we say it). *Content* is the information and message which a writer communicates. *Style* is the way in which this information is conveyed. These two halves of the whole embody, in a nutshell, the entire writing shebang. End of session.

Well, not quite. *Then* comes the matter of how to assemble these elements in such a way that they appeal to the imagination *and* provide food for the brain. In other words, to write both to inform and to entertain. Herein lies every writer's challenge—and herein lies the road to good literary style.

What exactly is style in writing? From one standpoint it is a kind of literary mating dance, complete with plumage spreads and mating calls, done by a writer to capture the readers' fleeting regard. Its objectives are three:

1. Gain the audience's attention
2. Hold their interest
3. Win their long-term confidence so that they *keep* reading.

From a more technical perspective, style is the way in which a writer uses language. Good style elevates writing above the level of hack journalism or industrial instructions. It's a way of combining the standard elements of prose—tone, vocabulary, rhythm, grammar, syntax, emphasis, usage—into a unified word tapestry which is amusing or lyrical or emotive or profound or fun. "Style," says Lord Chesterfield, "is the dress of thoughts."

Style, therefore, is the writer's personality reaching out to the reader from the one-dimensional page, "the Self escaping into the open," as E. B. White describes it, and as such, the attempt to enrich one's style, to hone it, ripen it, perfect it, is any thoughtful writer's life's aim.

And yet as with any skill, there are professional short cuts, formulas, axioms, and tricks of the trade that can prove *almost* as useful in the making of successful prose as long days and nights spent over the keyboard.

Here is a selection of these "tricks," most of them about style, a few about rewriting, problem solving, and, well, survival as a writer. Go through the pages that follow, chapter by chapter. Choose the entries that appeal to you and forget about those that don't. Some of the techniques presented here are familiar to most writers; some were passed on to me exclusively from writer friends; some are my own. All have helped me—and I think they will help you too.

Chapter

1

FINDING THE RIGHT WORD

E ACH word, as you are no doubt aware, even a word
  with many synonyms, has its own individual shade
of meaning that sets it apart from other words of its kind.
Knowledge of this semantic uniqueness—each word's
special color or flavor, if you wish to think of it in these
terms—is an essential ingredient in good writing and
should not be underestimated as a force for clear communication.

For example, take four words of similar definition:
Courageous, valiant, intrepid, and dauntless. All, of course,
have the same general meaning: brave. Yet each expresses
a different subtlety of emphasis. *Courageous* is brave, yes,
but it is a bravery most specifically of the spirit. A *valiant*
person is brave too, but in a kind of unselfishly heroic way
that adds a fine dignity to his or her endeavors. An *intrepid*
person is boldly brave, inexorably brave, perhaps with a
touch of the foolhearty thrown in as well. *Dauntless* persons may be valiant, may be intrepid; or they may not; we
do not know for sure. What we do know is that they will

3

never say die, and that their courage will persevere no matter what terrible obstacles stand in their way.

Four different words, four different meanings—and hence four different persons, four different situations, four different tales. Writing, when all is said and done, as Jonathan Swift once remarked, is really nothing more than "proper words in proper places." Here are some hints to help you put them there.

When in doubt, test the word in context before you use it.

While working on a novel, Gustave Flaubert is said to have spent days and sometimes weeks searching not only for the right word in a sentence but the perfect word—*le mot juste*. At times he rewrote passages fifty or sixty times, altering but a single word at each attempt. Flaubert once informed a friend that he knew when he had succeeded in finding *le mot juste* only when the thought of using any other word nauseated him.

Extreme perhaps, but remember, writing is nothing but words, and bottom line skillful writing, as Dean Swift reminds us, means nothing more than good words properly chosen and arranged. So choose carefully. Somewhere out there that precise word is always lurking, waiting for you, *calling* to you even. Ask yourself: Does this word's sound and sense precisely match my intended meaning? Does this word communicate what I really wish to say? Is there another word that will hit the nail more squarely on the head? What might it be?

Use invented and unusual words sparingly.

Some student writers use made-up or unusual—and therefore, they believe, "creative"—words. Archaic, neologistic, off-beat, ad hoc, onomatopoetic, and oddly juxtaposed and hyphenated words have their place in language, certainly. Just ask James Joyce and friends. But *only* in the right place—which is usually in creative fiction and poetry. In the domain of straight-ahead narrative such hybrids tend to stand out on the page like a forest of sore thumbs, serving more to stop the reader's eye than to accurately elucidate a point. Such words can be, if the brutal truth is told, a way of showing off.

Take the case of the fledgling author who, in an essay on his visit to France, describes a waiter at a greasy spoon–type restaurant as being "dog-pound dirty." No doubt the young writer is proud of this phrase, too proud to restrain himself from using it twice in the same composition. A bit of discretionary consideration, however, reveals that animal shelters and French restaurants are too tenuously linked to make real contextual or even poetic sense, and that a less contrived, more direct image, one that does not stand up on the page and say "look at me, look at me!" would be a good deal more appropriate.

In general, when searching for *le mot juste,* opt for the

5

clearest possible word. Leave the elliptical references to the poets and experimental fiction writers; at best, put them in reserve for that time when you are absolutely *sure* they belong.

Make sure the phrase fits the context.

Writers are notorious for letching after new, interesting turns of phrase. What worthy ink slinger would turn a cold shoulder to lines such as "a trombone and whiskey town"? Or "the irresistible thrill of loathing"? Or Edith Wharton's description of a society ball: "varnished barbarism"?

The problem is that while these and myriad other phrases look terrific out of context, they do not always fit the mood of the present sentence, paragraph, or page. When this occurs, the writer is obliged to make a hefty effort at self-control and save this pet verbal creation for a more appropriate time.

For example, if I describe a husky, slightly pretentious, and dippy middle-aged PTA president as being a "well-upholstered matron" this is an apt and picturesque turn of phrase. If I use the same term to characterize an obese, bewildered, elderly Oriental emigrant woman just off the boat from Cambodia, the phrase ceases to amuse. Ask yourself: Does the word fit the mood of the sentence? Is it in good taste? Does it synchronize with the sensibility of the subject as well as with the sound of the sentence? In short, is it appropriate?

You can give the word several other tests for appropriateness as well. Such as:

Say the word out loud in context several times.

If it feels off-target chances are it *is* off-target. If it feels right chances are it is right—*probably.* But only probably. The dilemma comes when several words seem correct and you have to choose among them. Reading aloud in this case will put you onto the scent and can even serve as an arbitration technique to make a final choice.

Write down each word and try it out in context.

Let us assume your aim is to describe a large, mysterious outcropping of rock in the desert. You wish to use two interesting adjectives to accomplish it. Jot down the adjectives under consideration and give each a trial run. For example:

"The canyon's single tower loomed ahead (immeasurable) (monumental), (epic), (colossal), (Atlantean), (leviathan-like), (skyscraper-like)
                              and
(immortal), (wondrous), (ancient), (invulnerable), (oracular), (abysmal), (silent).

Now cross out all the rejects. The final choices might characterize the rock as being:

7

- Monumental and invulnerable
- Epic and oracular
- Atlantean and silent
- Leviathan-like and ancient

If you are not immediately able to choose between the finalists, don't be afraid to leave them in place and come back later.

Use a tape recorder.

If you're really locked in a death grip with *le mot juste*, read the word in context into a tape recorder and listen carefully to how it sounds.

The advantage of using this method is that the playback takes the burden off the visual faculty and passes it onto the auditory—which is often a better judge of literary quality than the eye. Literature, after all, began with a spoken tradition and remains, many would agree, essentially an oral art.

Be aware of the difference between denotative words and connotative words.

A *denotative* word conveys information: "hat," "yellow," "twenty-five," "book," "cat," "big." Such words speak to the practicalist in us, to the data bank and statistician. A *connotative* word, on the other hand, is calculated to arouse emotional response, to give a fillip to imagination, to project a mood in our hearts and/or on our senses.

To denote a woman, I can refer to her as a "female," a "teacher," or a "customer." I can also speak of her as a "bimbo," a "maiden," or a "luminous creature," all connotative.

The distinction between denotative and connotative, then, is that connotative words express a writer's opinions and personal feelings while denotative words state the facts. As a careful writer, you will be aware of these subtle, yet significant, differences.

For example, if you refer to a person as being "tired" you convey a matter-of-fact, denotative message. If you describe the person as being "weary," the image becomes more personalized, as it does with the terms "drained" or "burned-out." These words are all synonyms, perhaps. Yet each carries a different degree of emotional charge. Be aware of what these charges are and use them knowingly. The following verse provides an astutely whimsical example of just how much connotations count, in life as well as in literature:

Call a woman a kitten, but never a cat;
You can call her a mouse, cannot call her a rat;
Call a woman a chick, but never a hen;
Or you surely will not be her caller again.

You can call her a duck, cannot call her a goose;
You can call her a deer, but never a moose;

9

You can call her a lamb, but never a sheep;
Economic she likes, but you can't call her cheap.

If you can't find the precise word, move on and come back to it later.

Most writers discover this trick on their own, especially if they write on deadlines. Better just to put an ✕ on the problem word, keep writing, and come back later. You'll bring a fresh eye to the decision then, and probably a fine solution.

Which brings up an important rule of thumb for writing practice in general: When your writing is going well, don't let *anything* stop your flow. *Don't* get hung up on the grammatical or factual details. Just leave them, get on with the brainstorming, finish the entire piece, *then* return to fix the fine points.

Tips on using a thesaurus and/or a word finder.

A thesaurus, or word finder, is a writer's best friend, more helpful than the dictionary, really. Yet it is a strangely undervalued and underconsulted reference source. Some amateurs and professionals, amazingly, consider using a thesaurus "cheating," that not finding the exact word on your own is a creative cop-out.

Nonsense. We write to communicate the best we can:

the final product is also the final score, at least as far as the reader is concerned, and any legitimate aid that helps improve our finished literary product is fair and square. So testifies Honoré de Balzac, who spoke for all great writers when he said, "I take my work wherever I find it." Make use of *all* your resources.

Here are some tips for using word-finding references:

- Consult the thesaurus before you begin a particular project and compile a representative list of the kinds of words you expect to use. For example, if you are preparing an essay on modern sculpture, you'll know in advance that you will need plenty of synonyms for words such as "statue," "art," and "sculptor." Look them up now. If you are writing about dogs, compile a list of canine synonyms, then refer to the list as you write. This trick will save you lots of time plus the annoyance of constantly reaching for the reference book.

- Pay attention to the slang items, colloquialisms, and foreign phrases in each entry. Occasionally a foreignism or colloquialism will suit your needs better than a conventional word.

- Read the word lists in a thesaurus or word finder *slowly.* Rapid scanning saves time, perhaps, but you can lose plenty of fish off your hook in the process. Go over each choice thoughtfully, carefully, sounding it out as you do. Consider it,

11

ponder it, roll it on the tongue. Slowly, slowly is the best approach.

• If you're searching for dated or "period" words from, say, the 1920s or 1930s, consult an older word-finding reference. *Roget's Thesaurus,* for instance, has been published in the United States steadily since 1911 (qualifying it as a record of philological evolution as well as a writer's friend). Older copies of *Roget's* can be found in libraries or secondhand book stores.

• If you write with a word processor, think about purchasing a thesaurus program. And don't be put off by past disappointments in this department. Though early word-finder programs were less than comprehensive, today's more powerful machines have changed all that, and a good computer thesaurus now has almost as many words in it as an unabridged *Roget's.*

Chapter

2

TONE

TONE is the personal attitude writers bring to their work. Just as in music a note has a specific pitch that characterizes it as a C or a D sharp, so a writer's work has its own distinguishing sound as well. This sound can be joyous or self-important; it can be bland, aloof, scientific, tongue-in-cheek—you name it. Inappropriate tone tends to confuse and finally to repel readers: just as a dull tone bores them, a self-righteous tone angers them. "The most difficult task for a writer is to get the right 'voice' for his material," claims the writer, John Fowles. "By voice I mean the overall impression one has of the creator behind what he creates."

Careful writers are aware of this fact, and they mold their tone to conform to their listener's ear.

Write to the specific audience you are addressing.

If you are penning an essay on a rock band for a school newspaper, then a colloquial, freewheeling tone is fine. If you are designing a letter to your graduating class to solicit donations, a friendly, candid tone is appropriate. If you are writing a PhD in linguistics, a more formal tone is called for.

All this sounds obvious. Yet it is surprising how many writers err in their assessments of an audience's psychological level, maintaining a rigidly similar tone whether they are addressing children or professors or hobos. This problem can be avoided by first asking oneself a few revealing questions:

- Who exactly am I writing to?
- What general age group do they belong to?
- What are their interests? Educational levels? Social backgrounds?
- Exactly *why* will they be reading this piece, and what will they hope to get from it?

Try picturing your readers. Imagine them looking over your manuscript and evaluating it. Who are they? What do they look like? What tone will be most pleasing to them? What will it take to get them to listen to what you have to say? What kind of tone should you *not* use?

Assess the above items honestly; the right tone will then come automatically.

Be personable.

It could be argued that if there is a single personality trait most necessary for public success it is likability. Politicians, movie stars, sometimes even sports heros, all excite an impulse in us to know them, to speak with them, to be their friends. The same process is required for successful writing too, only here the sense of likability is projected not via charisma but through the way written ideas are expressed. And further: authors must not only come across as being likable themselves but, simultaneously, they must present the impression that they *like the reader*, that they think the reader is an intelligent, special person, that they know of his or her inner concerns, that they are here to address these concerns—and that they care.

How is such an intimate bond forged? In many ways.

One author does it with humor: "You can add thyme to the eggs if you like while they're frying (personally I can't stand the stuff)."

Another does it by anticipating the reader's needs: "Place two drops of oil on the slide. Careful now, the oil tends to drip and stain."

Another is attentive: "Is the lace tight enough? Satisfied? Okay, now tie the other with a good sharp pull."

Still another wins approval with modesty: "I would like to sound learned on this point, of course, but the truth is that I am more ignorant of the Hundred Years War than most school children."

Make yourself likeable by asking the reader questions: "Jack E. Leonard—remember him?"

By sympathizing with the reader: "By now you are no doubt overloaded with warnings concerning the curious workings of this enzyme."

By projecting warmth and emotion: "My heart and tendons alike ached for the old coolies as they shouldered bales that would cause most young men to stagger."

By caring: "Patients will often find that a pillow doubled over twice is far more supportive and comfortable than one simply propped up."

All in all, writers make themselves likeable in the same way we all do: by being friendly, interesting, and genuinely concerned with the welfare of the person we are talking to. "When we encounter a natural style," writes Blaise Pascal, "we are always surprised and delighted, for we thought to see an author and instead found a man."

**Keep the tone on an even keel from
beginning to end.**

If you start out writing in a formal tone, continue in this way from beginning to end. Don't suddenly lapse into slapstick or become overly familiar in the middle of a factual piece. Such a shift in tone will confuse readers. It will make you as writer appear uncertain and inconsistent.

Similarly, avoid sudden, qualitative drops or raises in language level. For instance, a vulgarism, even a mild one, thrown into an otherwise formal text can cause a disastrous ripple to spread throughout your work. Joking at the wrong time does the same, as do injections of abrasive opinion, sudden explosions of self-righteous anger, out-of-place sexual innuendos. Tone, in writing, is another word for taste, and taste that swings between extremes is often poor taste.

Beware the "trumpeter" effect.

Writers who insist on calling frequent attention to themselves eventually become irksome. Typical cases:

> "As I have already made quite clear several times throughout this text. . . ."
> "As I myself was the first to disprove Lazlow's hypothesis, it seems only fair for me now to go on record as saying that I believe. . . ."
> "This colorful quarter-note refrain—which yours truly championed years before they'd heard of Miles Davis—remains a classic. . . ."

In general, readers will like you better and respect what you say more willingly if you as author remain a pleasant, soft-spoken voice behind the scenes. This means writing in the first-person only when it's really necessary and avoiding boasting or dogmatism or a patronizing tone. It also means eliminating apologetic disclaimers and musings on your own insufficiency—these too quickly cloy.

You as writer know what you are writing about. You are an expert in your field. It is your right, nay, your duty, to sound authoritative and able. So let your competence shine through, not by calling attention to yourself, but by saying what you have to say wisely and well.

Don't tell your readers—show them.

Many beginning writers make this cardinal error: They describe their thoughts, feelings, and attitudes about a subject rather than allowing the facts, action, and evidence to speak for themselves.

You can, for example, tell me that "Robert is feeling sad." You can also *show* me by writing that: "Robert moped up the stairs."

You can tell me that "The ship was heavily weighted." You can *show* me by writing: "Excess cargo made her tilt slightly to port." A picture is worth a thousand words.

Persuade with examples, not opinions.

The best method for making readers see things from your perspective is to present so much hard evidence and so

many persuasive examples that they will reach your conclusions on their own. In this way readers are flattered
into thinking they have figured it all out for themselves,
and you appear all the more modest and intelligent for
having gently pointed the way. This is a refinement of the
"show me, don't tell me" principle.

Here's a good instance of what I'm talking about. A
reporter for a small financial journal in Washington re-
cently wrote that:

> the American automotive labor force has become increas-
> ingly slug-like and inept during the past three decades.
> Clearly, it is not keeping up either with the German
> competition or the Japanese juggernaut. This, it seems
> to me, is a reflection of prevailing mugwump attitudes
> existing not only in the automotive industry but
> throughout the entire American work place, yet another
> gloomy indicator of the American laborer's current ob-
> session with the fast buck and the "avoid hard work at all
> costs" syndrome. Indeed, if we do not become more
> heedful of this decline, we may soon slip to a dismal
> number three status in world industrial production, if
> not lower. It's time we all woke up, shed our smug
> attitudes about being "Number One," and faced the
> bloody facts—American economy is slipping, and badly.

Fine. That's this fellow's opinion. But is he telling us
the real story? We don't know for sure because besides
scolding us for our indolence and giving us some hand-
wringing predictions, he has failed to provide solid evidence. Nor do his strong-arm terms such as "obsession,"

21

"slug-like," "bloody facts," and "mugwump" win us over. Such peevish jargon usually makes readers uncomfortable and more than a little suspicious. The writer has, in short, given us his feelings but not the facts.

Another reporter, this one on the staff of a Wisconsin financial newsletter, makes a similar point. But here, using hard information to back up her thesis, she lets the information sell itself. She writes:

> In the past several decades American auto production has surrendered 37% of its variant market share to the Japanese. Fluctuations occur, of course, but the major thrust has been towards a percentage drop each year since 1970. Job absenteeism at the Ford and Chevrolet plant, meanwhile, has mushroomed by over 5 percent per annum. This is a particularly ominous sign because, as you know, absenteeism in Japan is an almost unknown phenomenon. Hundreds of Americans polled on this subject express alarm over this perilous situation; yet, according to *The New York Times:* 'Increased manufacturing production and the improvement of worker incentives remain surprisingly low on this year's voter's priority list.' The research company of Manning and Jones predicts that, given the present decline in sales, by the year 2000 the American auto industry will control less than 10% of the world's automotive business. And that's pretty scary!

Flatter your reader.

Read the first of the two preceding sample paragraphs. The writer is angry and guilt-mongering. He makes us feel that the decline of the American work ethic is some-how our fault, and that without doubt we are all doomed. We certainly don't feel any better after having read this outburst, nor do we particularly like its author. As a result, we are probably not going to pay much attention to what he has to say either.

The second sample paragraph produces an entirely different effect. The author's assumption that we have a certain political sophistication; that we are familiar with terms like "variant market share"; that we are already informed of pertinent facts ("as you know, absenteeism in Japan is an almost unknown phenomenon")—all this flatters us and makes us feel perceptive and competent.

After presenting the news in a concise and efficient way, moreover, her ending line—"and that's pretty scary"—is surprising and endearing, a human counter-balance to the relentless statistics that have come before. The author is not scolding us, not lecturing us. Yet we are more anxious to take action from her words than from the reprimand by the first author. Why? Because the second author has treated us as her equals.

Whenever you wish to write convincing prose, address your readers as intelligent, informed peers. Your readers may not in fact be intelligent or informed, but that's their problem. Your problem is to make them think that they are. In this manner you win readers' good will and at the same time advance them toward seeing things the way you see them, for it is an established fact that we believe those people we like far more readily than those we dislike.

Address the reader directly.

Use the word "you" whenever possible. Instead of penning such windy phrases as "One will discover that . . ."
say "You will discover that. . . ." Instead of announcing
how the mythical "reader" should "note such and so" or
"recall that so and so did this and that," say, "You will
note that . . ." or "You will recall that. . . ."

The "you" technique accomplishes what is perhaps the
single most important task in all writing—involving the
reader. Use it whenever you can. It is especially effective
in colloquial writing and in works that concentrate on
instruction, persuasion (especially ad copy), and self-help.

Avoid stating things negatively.

A philosopher once suggested that Germanic philosophy
tends to be so pessimistic because the Germanic language
places such a large number of gratuitous *nein's* at the end
of its sentences: "It's good, no." "You're happy, no."

A wicked exaggeration, no doubt. Still, from a psychological standpoint it is clearly the case that our psyches
prefer affirmation to disaffirmation. They prefer to learn
what *did* happen, not what didn't.

Consequently it is more or less an accepted axiom
among writers that when you can state a negative fact
positively, *do so.* Strunk and White in *The Elements of Style,*
as often, say it best: "Use the word *not* as a means of denial
or in antithesis, never as a means of evasion."

Some simple examples:

NEGATIVE PHRASING: "He was not good enough."
BETTER: "He was inadequate."

NEGATIVE PHRASING: "His hands were not clean."
BETTER: "His hands were dirty."

NEGATIVE PHRASING: "Rover was not good."
BETTER: "Rover was bad."

Chapter

3

TRICKS FOR MORE EXPRESSIVE, COLORFUL WRITING

BECAUSE good writing is also colorful writing, writers are ever on the lookout for the verbal rare bird, the unpredictable exposure, the slight turn of phrase that makes what's been said a thousand times suddenly gleam again. Ezra Pound was fond of quoting himself to young poets, and he repeated it over and over: "Make it new."

Precisely how to make it new cannot be reduced to formulas, though Lord knows many people have tried. What *can* be reduced, or rather deduced, are principles— "tricks" we are calling them here—of expressive writing which we can then interpret in our own work.

Keep it specific.

Don't say dog. Say cocker spaniel. Don't say house. Say cottage. Or vicarage. Or split-level. Or shack. Avoid general statements filled with lackluster parts of speech.

Be concrete whenever you can. It's not a fighter plane; it's an "F16." Don't announce that "the visitor ate a big meal." Entertain me with the particulars: "The exhausted stranger devoured a half a turkey and a mug of stout."

A mist that "curls" around a boat is more intriguing than one that simply "covers" it. Learning that the birds "warbled listlessly" tells me more about what happened that day in the woods then hearing that the birds "sang." A piano that sits in the middle of a room "glowing from a rubdown of cactus oil" is a piano I won't soon forget. Whenever you can, bring your readers into the action. Transport them to the scene on the magic carpet of details. Be specific.

Use words that evoke images.

The more visually oriented a piece of descriptive writing is, the better it transmits an author's intent. "The green cabin by the fork in Prescott's road" is received by the imagination with more enthusiasm and greater retentiveness than "the house along the street." "A smoking pyramid of neatly severed legs and shoulders" makes a far more graphic impression than "a pile of dismembered bodies."

In the following examples, note how the concrete, visually oriented sentences convey a miniworld of atmosphere and implication, and how the general sentences, devoid of such imagery, fall flat.

General	Concrete
I tripped and fell to the ground.	I tripped on a stump, flew through the air, and landed on my whoopsy-doodle.
I hitched a ride to the city on a truck.	I thumbed a ride with an army convoy truck into Denver.
My back is sore all over.	I ache along every nerve ending and vertebra of my spine.

If the experiences of Jim Hawkins and David Balfour, of Kim, of Nostromo, have seemed for the moment real to countless readers, if in reading Carlyle we have almost the sense of being present at the taking of the Bastille, it is because the details used are definite, the terms concrete. It is not that every detail is given—that would be impossible as well as to no purpose—but that all the significant details are given, and with such accuracy and vigor that the reader, in imagination, can project himself into the scene. [1]

Let others speak for you.

Once you've made your argument, let others back it up—and embellish it—via illustrations and examples. Note the following paragraph, how it strikes its point, then strengthens its argument with a rich array of illustrative supports:

[1] Strunk & White, p. 17.

The critic Arnould maintained that Celmens was not an artist at all, not even "worthy of the plagiarist's name," that he was a false literary prophet; that he was, as De Verre similarly observed, "a self-invented Saltimbanque come to play Messieur Poseur de belles lettres." Of course, Arnould was speaking from personal jealousy as well as professional bitter grapes. Ten years earlier Celmens had engaged Arnould's wife in a searing *tête-à-tête* that was the talk of Lyons, and which had caused Le Loup to quip famously that "No woman is safe from an intelligent male." A popular story was just then going the rounds during this famed tryst wherein the Reverend Abernathe confronted Sir Lionel Scofield, claiming that Scofield was such a scoundrel that it was a tossup whether he would die on the gallows or of the pox, and whereby Scofield replied that this matter depended entirely on whether he, Scofield, embraced Abernathe's "principles or his mistress." Now, however, the names Abernathe and Scofield in the story were replaced to read Arnould and Celmens.

Here the author uses a lively pastiche of quotation, anecdote, aphorism, catty gossip, and historical example to sustain his main narrative. The result is that we are entertained while we are educated.

Insert colorful observations and examples into your work whenever you can. It's the stuff of top-notch prose. Additions that add zest to any paragraph include:

- Quotes and quotations.
- Parenthetical asides.
- Jokes and humorous stories.

- Anecdotes and tales.
- Case histories.
- Testimonials.
- Statistics and interesting facts.
- Aphorisms, proverbs, sayings, witticisms.
- Bulleted items (as here).

The best thing about these examples is that they take you off the hot seat and let others speak in your place. They are a kind of author's freebee that helps add stylistic variety to your prose, provides a diversion for the reader, and, best of all, invokes the voice of outside authority to bolster whatever point you are making.

Let others make you sound good.

Similarly, but with an emphasis on quotations and aphorisms, there are few devices that make prose scintillate more than amusing, appropriate, and/or wise literary citations.

Here I am, writing on how a certain friend is overanxious to pay off a debt. At just the right moment I call in Francois de la Rochefoucauld, the greatest of court wits, to remind my readers that "our excessive eagerness in paying off an obligation can be a form of ingratitude."

Here I am, ready to argue a historical dilemma. Before I begin I warn the reader, with thanks to Matthew Arnold, about "that huge Mississippi of falsehood called history."

Here I am, musing on what I've learned from my recent trip to China. "The further one travels," I (and Lao Tzu) write, "the less one understands."

Let the great thinkers and wits and poets and mystics say it for you. They'll do it well, and you'll look good for having invoked such appropriate mentors.

Write with dynamic verbs.

I can tell you about the young girl who "walked" across the street. It's more informative *and* colorful if I tell you that she "ambled" across or "shuffled" or "loped." Perhaps I simply "ate" my breakfast this morning. An observant writer would also note that I "wolfed" my breakfast down. I "scolded" my teenage son last night. It could also be said that I "tongue-lashed" him, "lectured" him, "screeched" at him, even "yammered" at him. Yes, I "grow" a garden, but more to the point, I "nurture" it. Note:

Generic verb	Dynamic verb
run	race, dart, sprint, whiz
make	fashion, construct, forge, frame
carry	transport, deliver, convey, lug
hit	strike, cuff, pommel, thwack
read	study, peruse, pore over, wade through
speak	converse, chat, utter, orate

These are arbitrary examples, of course, and you will want to improvise in your own ways. The idea to keep in mind is that verbs come in two forms, the generic and the specific. The generic, the garden variety verb, says it as it is: "see," "take," "kill," "like." The specific verb then hones in on an aspect of the generic and gives it dynamism and character: "gaze," "grab," "slaughter," "savor." Both forms have their place. But for vibrant, forceful language, use a predominance of vibrant, forceful verbs.

Choose action over exposition.

Expository writing is explanatory writing. It is used to convey information and facts. An encyclopedia is composed of expository prose. So is an almanac.

While exposition is necessary to some degree in any work of fiction or nonfiction, it is usually the least colorful form of prose. You can often replace it with its more entertaining and more animated counterpart, action narrative.

In the following lines the writer employs expository writing to convey information about a character's appearance and personality:

"Ralph was a diminutive, exquisite, irritable little man who was obsessed with his appearance, especially his pomaded hairdo, and who was forever plotting ways to insult his coworkers."

A perfectly respectable piece of prose. But try conveying the same information via action writing, and Ralph

35

ceases to be a package of descriptions and turns into a human being:

"Ralph smoothed his pomaded hair back for the fourth time. He glanced at his tiny figure in the mirror, picked an infinitesimally small piece of thread off his lapel, and whispered to his reflection: 'You're looking particularly blue and *bloated* this morning, Dear.'

" 'Oh yes!' he suddenly shouted. 'That's a *heavenly* line. I'll use it on that slug, Ingrid, the *second* I get to the office.' "

Another example, this one from a scholarly piece of writing on early Christianity. Though the form is different, the same principle applies:

"The idea of a fusion of philosophies and religions led to the founding of Gnosticism which for its tenets drew upon Philo, the mystery religions, and many other sources, including the revelations of Jesus. The result was, the early Christians founders announced, a heresy, and they combatted it with all the theological arguments at their command.

Fine. Another piece of solid expo. But by placing more emphasis on action writing, the paragraph can be improved:

"Take a goodly helping of Philo and Plato's philosophies, mix it with several Greek and Roman mystery religions, add a half-dozen secret mystical teachings, now lost, plus some revelations of Jesus Christ—and you have Gnosticism. The early Christian fathers counted this heathen rival as a public enemy and were continually devising ingenious theological arguments to suppress it."

Use parallelism when you wish to create emphasis and rhythm.

Parallelism means presenting two, three, or more parts of a sentence in the same grammatical form, for effect or to express ideas of equal importance:

> "If life allows, if the good Lord's willing, if the creek don't rise, I'll be there tomorrow morn at eight sharp."

> "The night was dark, the moon white, the wind still, the leaves twisting silently on their branches."

> "Speak softly and carry a big stick."

The aesthetic part of the human psyche is almost magically affected by rhythm, repetition, equilibrium, and the unity of balanced parts. Indeed, the power and persuasive impact which many political and commercial slogans produce is due to their use of parallel construction. Witness:

> "Had enough? Vote Republican!"

> "A chicken in every pot, a car in every garage."

". . . that this government of the people, by the people, for the people, shall not perish from the earth."

Parallelism allows writers to state their ideas rapidly, intensely, economically. It adds a pleasant strength and meter to prose. Imagine, for instance, if Teddy Roosevelt had warned, "You should speak softly while you are carrying a big stick." Removing the imperative from the second part of the sentence, a relatively small modification in itself, robs the entire phrase of its memorable music. Though its meaning remains exactly the same as before, the symmetry of the two contrasting ideas has been ruptured, and herein lies the difference.

Write in the present and/or simple past tense whenever possible.

Here are some examples:

"He is going to ask."
BETTER: "He will ask."

"Sorry that I have been disappointing you."
BETTER: "Sorry I disappointed you."

"It was in the process of being completed."
BETTER: "It was almost complete."

In general, keep your verbs as short and as unencumbered by auxiliaries as possible. "Wished" is less cumbersome than "had wished." "Will have wished" is even more top-heavy. These double and triple whammies should raise red flags and should usually (usually, I say, as there are always exceptions) be shortened.

Write colloquially whenever you can.

Colloquial means conversational, not slang, as some people believe. The way you and I would talk if we were sitting together having dinner or speaking on the phone, that's colloquial style.

The qualities which characterize this important genre are as follows:

1. Common use of clipped words (cop, phone, TV); idioms (come hell or high water, down-and-dirty); and simplified grammar.
2. A nonscholarly vocabulary.
3. Frequent contractions such as "we'll" for "we will" or "shouldn't" for "should not."
4. A familiar, personal, occasionally intimate tone.
5. Relatively short, pithy sentences which are sometimes grammatically incomplete. (This book, as you've noticed, is largely an amalgam of the colloquial and the slightly more conventional "informal" styles.)

Generally speaking, unless a writer is hemmed in by the inexorable dictates of highly formal writing, as in a

master's thesis or an article for a medical journal, colloquial is the voice of choice.

Why? Because this writing style allows an author el-
bow room (a colloquial phrase) for colorful expression and
creative tangenting (a colloquial neologism). This, in
turn, speaks more fluently to readers than the starched,
scholarly tones of formal prose (slightly wise-guy colloquial). Again, don't think you're slaughtering the King's
English (idiomatic expression) by writing colloquially.
You're not (colloquial use of a contraction). Many magazines, sometimes even the highbrow ones (colloquial adjective) such as *Harpers* and *The Atlantic* are chock-full
(colloquial idiom) of colloquial writing. That's one reason
they're so popular, in fact—because they make "serious"
subjects palatable to the reader.

The secret of writing accents.

Many years ago when the Broadway show *Brigadoon* was
in rehearsal, a voice coach was brought in to teach the
performers a Scottish accent. While the performers
learned their lessons quickly, a problem soon arose: in the
early run-throughs no one could understand what they
were saying: "Whisht, ma' lord, a' gaes wrang when the
Master's oot; but ay, I'll take care o' the ruckle wi' ye
ma'self." It took a second, wiser coach to point out that
stage accents should present the *illusion,* not the reality of
foreign pronunciation, and that accenting every ninth or

tenth word in a passage is all that's necessary to convey the impression of native speaking.

This lesson transposes itself to the art of writing as well. Accents can do much to create character and authenticity, yes. But only when used like polka dots on a top hat—sparingly. Thus, rather than quote an Italian immigrant who begs off an invitation by saying: "I donna' think I'm agonna' be able ta come'a to yeh house tonight a' fah' dinner," reduce it to one or two accented (and readable) words: "I don't think I'm agonna' be able to come to your house tonight a' for dinner."

Consult authors who specialize in ethnic characters or specific historical periods. An excellent East Indian accent, for instance, can be found in Kipling's *Kim*. Good Cockney voices are plentiful in Kipling's *Soldier's Three*. Scottish accents of all varieties are found in Sir Walter Scott's novels, especially in *The Bride of Lammermoor*. Edgar Allen Poe's *The Gold Bug* offers a remarkably accurate model of a nineteenth-century Southern black's accent.

Reach one extra notch for the surprising and unexpected word or phrase.

Writers are often tempted to settle for the respectable at the expense of the excellent. This means that all babies are "cherubic," all starlets "breathless," all mathematical solutions "elegant," all harmonious happenings "resonant," all stalled situations "entropic," all oversensitive people "brittle"—not entirely cliches, any of them, but here lies the trap. These and a thousand other interesting, hard-working words are just uncommon enough to fool the writer into thinking that he or she is being original.

In truth, we have heard these phrases before. Not a thousand times, maybe, not even a hundred times. But definitely before. They are not the stuff that first-rate prose is made of; they by no means deliver those perfectly descriptive yet entirely unanticipated images that force readers to see the subject fresh and new. To accomplish this, you must reach one rung higher, one inch farther. "Carefully examined," writes Ford Madox Ford, "a good—an interesting—style will be found to consist in a consistent succession of tiny, unobservable surprises."

Examples of such surprising—and hence powerful— writing are endless. Here are several:

- John Buchan tells us that in one of Sir Walter Scott's novels: "the sense of marching fatality is unbroken by the awkwardness of invention."

  "Marching fatality"—what an inexorable and disquieting description of life! It makes us realize that our *own* fate is also on the march. And the "awkwardness" of invention. Ordinarily we think of invention as being creative and ingenious, cer- tainly anything but awkward. Yet invention when inappropriate can, we realize thanks to the au- thor's sharp phrasing, be as ungainly as anything imagined by Don Quixote or Rube Goldberg.

- Josephine Tey tells us that the stars "merely reduce one to the status of an amoeba." But a snow-covered mountain? This, says Ms. Tey, is "a nice human-sized yardstick."

  Amoeba-like—an apt and disquieting imagery for humanity's cosmic insignificance. We do indeed stand to the stars as protozoans. Yet it takes a clever writer's eye to see things this way, then quickly to soothe the reader's ego with the reminder of "human-sized" snowy peaks.

- Here is Richard Hughes at his best describing a hurricane in *A High Wind in Jamaica:* "Through the gaping frames the lightning-lit scene without was visible. The creepers, which before had looked like cobwebs, now streamed up into the sky like new-combed hair. Bushes were lying flat, laid back on the ground as close as a rabbit lays back his ears. Branches were leaping about loose in the sky. . . . The bouncing rain seemed to cover the ground with a white smoke. . . .

  "Lightning-lit," creepers like "cobwebs" and "new-combed hair," "bouncing rain"—powerful, fresh, imagistic writing at its best.

- Another evocatively clever use of descriptive phrases is found in this passage from Jonathan Carroll's *Sleeping in Flame:*

Tall, topped with thick black hair, eyes set wide apart, lips round and perfect as a dark coin. Ingram (Maris

called him "Inky") was thin and dressed in typical L.A.
wear—T-shirt with the name "MEAT PUPPETS" across
the front—baggy/fashionable pants, sneakers. He talked
fast but his hands never moved except to bring the hot-
dog to his mouth. I kept imagining him at a radio
microphone with those still hands, fielding questions
from guys selling real estate on the Lost Continent of
Atlantis (once it rose).

Chapter

4

USEFUL STYLISTIC TRICKS

O F these there are legion, and every writer will develop a few of his or her own. Here is a selection to get you started.

After making a strategic or dramatic point, move away from your subject for a moment, then return with sudden force.

First you introduce the topic. Then you shift to a second and seemingly unrelated idea. Finally you return to the original subject with a sudden force that ties both thoughts together into a single, high-impact unity. Here are two examples of this effective technique.

"In the past centuries these seemingly quiet volcanos, which many falsely believe are extinct, have claimed countless lives. Visitors come here weekly to vacation. Sensible visitors, telephone operators from

Houston, TV repairmen from Ohio. Little do they know that when they walk the streets of Loa Koa they are treading on the bones of a hundred thousand agonized dead."

"Promoted? To Colonel?" The words burned in his head. He lay in ambivalent silence for a moment. The sparrows on the windowsill quarreled loudly. He wondered what they were quarreling about. "I can't make sense of it, Crawford," he finally said in a whisper. "I can't picture myself wearing all them stars and stripes."

Three ways to keep your reader emotionally involved:

1. Present a mystery, then unravel it in stages. This technique is by no means confined to novels and in fact can become the very backbone of a gripping piece of reportorial prose: What is this mysterious force that keeps the electron circling around the proton? What caused this seemingly well-adjusted teenager to turn to drugs? How could a boy of Chatterton's age ever write such profound poetry? What can the besieged gardener do to combat Japanese beetles?

2. Create a situation of jeopardy, then resolve it. A critic once remarked that the essence of any drama is as follows: In the first act you chase your hero up a tree; in the second you throw stones at him; in the third you get him down. This principle, so universal and so recognizable, applies to other branches of writing as well. In the first part of the text you establish the trouble point: the police are stymied by a criminal syndicate; the orange crop in California is undergoing a new, mysterious blight. In the second act, the middle part of the essay, you develop the problem and present the dramatic particulars: the crime, it turns out, is linked to international terrorism; scientists are working on several ingenious approaches at once to control the blight. Finally, you reach a resolution, usually one that gives your reader a sense of closure: the crime is solved; the blight is controlled.

3. *Identify a problem that readers are personally experiencing, then help them overcome it.* Perhaps your readers are single parents looking for ways to amuse their children. Tell them how. Perhaps readers want to improve their tennis serve. Give them some tips. You, I, everyone reads with the same basic question: What's in this for me? Entertainment? Instruction? Inspiration? Emotional comfort? Laughs? Whatever the impression you wish to make, there must always be a payoff to it, always *some* way in which it fulfills a reader's needs. You as writer must determine what these needs are, these problems, these yearnings and emotional gaps—and fill them.

**Introduce a humorous or dramatic motif,
   then use it later with an ironic twist.**

A story opens with a man lying in a hospital bed. Extremely upset, he is gazing at the patterns on the ceiling.

49

Since he was a boy, he tells us, he has discovered that studying the cracks in the ceiling can be strangely and hypnotically comforting for him. Later on the man is visited in the hospital by a friend. The friend tells him something provocative, but the man does not reply. The friend is annoyed: "What's the matter, Lee?" he asks. "Answer me, for God's sake. You look as if you're more interested in the ceiling than in what I'm saying!"

Use action to make a significant point.

The old "Don't tell me, show me" rule again. In this case, show them with dynamic imagery and motion rather than exposition.

ORDINARY: Horst was very surprised.
BETTER: Horst let out a long, low whistle.

ORDINARY: In the Grand Empire the church was becoming a less important public authority than the state.
BETTER: In the Grand Empire the church lost its position as public authority when the State swooped down and usurped its major policy-making functions.

ORDINARY: When Hitler learned that Paris had surrendered, he and his generals became overjoyed.
BETTER: When Hitler learned that Paris had surrendered, he danced a jaunty jig in front of his ecstatic generals.

Use a series of short sentences to build tension.

In the right place—which is usually a moment of tense action—a series of terse sentences strung together with heavy emphasis on the verbs will increase intensity and build drama. Witness:

> "It was cracked and it was missing several gems. But it was usable. She raised it gingerly above her head, closed her eyes, grimaced, and made the third pass. Then she put the wand down. And waited. Nothing. Quiet. Then—something? A noise by the banister? A whimper in the corner of the room? She couldn't be sure. Wait! It was a whimper. And a terrible one!"

> "The signal to advance was given. But the lieutenants on Blucher's flank refused to charge. Why? No one was sure. Communications between the command and flank were nonexistent. Why? No one knew that either. No one knew anything. Except that Napoleon's dragoons were coming hard on the terrier's far post and were pressing Andre and Brunwitz on both flanks. Hard. And firing ball from three directions. What could be done? No one knew."

Use irony.

Irony, in a nutshell, is the discrepancy between appearance and reality, between what seems to be happening

51

and what actually *is* happening. For instance, the condemned man who turns to his executioner and says, "A
great day for an execution, isn't it?" is being ironic. He
means just the opposite. Yet in this short speech a world
of information comes to us about the condemned. We see
the man's courage and composure, his humor in the face
of catastrophe, his way with words. We like him; we hope
he will be spared. Understatement, overstatement, exaggeration, sarcasm, satire—all are forms of irony which
when rightly used can work on two levels simultaneously,
revealing important layers of meaning beneath the words
themselves.

In John O'Hara's short story "Pipe Night," poignancy
and humor are derived from a kind of on-going, implicit
ironic joke that runs through the entire piece like mock-
ing background music. The story is set at an all-male
gathering held in a Rotarian club-like banquet hall where
one of the members is delivering a remembrance speech
for a newly deceased club mate. The trouble is that the
longer the speaker drones on extolling the "virtues" of the
dearly departed the clearer it becomes to us, the readers,
that the deceased was one of most humdrum, most vac-
uous nonentities ever to walk God's green earth. Each
attempt made by the well-meaning speaker to put his
friend in a favorable light, each time he describes the
man's personality and accomplishments, the dead mem-
ber's deficiencies become that much more apparent to
us—and presumably to the other club members as well.
Ironically, the speaker's very attempt to eulogize his
friend turns out to be a kind of denunciation.

This is irony at its best. On the surface the narrative appears to be saying one thing while on a level immediately below quite another meaning is implied, usually in direct contradiction to the first. The possibilities inherent in such a device for creating humor, conflict, and psychological revelation are endless. Here are a few further examples:

"The young man turned to him with a disarming candor which put him on his guard immediately."

"Oh, they were a choice, beautiful lot those guards, muscled, ruthless, without conscience—just what was needed to keep the population of starving orphans and dying old people from violently overthrowing the state."

"Seven-year old Nicholas was chosen to lay the last brick in the school science building ceremony because he was brilliant, handsome, perceptive, a wonderful student, a remarkable person—and because he was the only child in the fifth grade tall enough to get a brick onto the top of the wall."

Be careful using the dash.

In the nineteenth century writers tended to use the semicolon practically to death. Today the dash has usurped its popularity, becoming so popular in newspaper and magazine writing that it has encouraged the development of a kind of jerky, half-finished writing style all its own.

You've seen examples. Every few lines a dash appears. No matter if it's grammatically correct—writers invent their own rules as they go along. After a while—for sure—the page starts to look like a racing form—if you can read it at all.

Dashes, properly speaking, are used to mark unexpected turns of thought, to introduce an afterthought or repetitive phrase, or to set off material that is too short to be placed in parentheses. It is a powerful piece of punctuation but can be quickly rendered impotent and even distracting by overexposure. Be especially careful of using the dash as a constant separator of clauses, as if it were a kind of halfhearted semicolon. This will weaken your prose.

Vary the lengths of your sentences and paragraphs.

Writers are weavers, and sentences are their threads. After several long sentences use a short one. After several short ones, a long one. Then a medium. Then two shorties. Keep varying the length and rhythm of word combinations. Throw in a single word now and then. Or a short question. After it place a winding, several-claused sentence as counterpoint.

Ditto for paragraphs. Too many long paragraphs appear forbidding. Too many short ones seem superficial. If your paragraphs all tend to run approximately the same lengths, your readers will become bored. Keep varying things.

It's not that people consciously notice sentence or paragraph lengths. It's subliminal, but nonetheless very real. Such elements are among the so-called "indefinables" that are responsible for the production of good writing, and bad.

Avoid frequent repetition of a character's name; identify him or her with a pronoun or descriptive phrase.

Few things are more annoying than the overuse of a name. Note: "Then *John* reached for the matches. *John* knew that the wind would be coming up soon. 'Yes,' he thought. 'I'll need a fire within the hour.' But the sun was already setting and *John* was having difficulty seeing his knapsack."

Avoid this irritation by varying names and descriptions of people. Note some of the many ways you can describe your characters:

Description	Example
Pronoun	"Yes," (John) he replied.
Profession	"Yes," (John) the *old window wiper* replied.
Nationality	"Yes," (John) *the lanky Greek* replied.
Appearance	"Yes," (John) *the tanned, muscle-bound kid* replied.

Character	"Yes," (John) *the saintly man* replied.
Title	"Yes," (John) the *Lord High Poobah* replied.
Accomplishment	"Yes," (John) the *three-time winner* replied.
Species	"Yes," (John) *the little fish* replied.
Present mood	"Yes," (John) the *now-peeved grocer* replied.
Present physical position	"Yes," (John) the *reclining child* replied.
Present physical condition	"Yes," (John) the *nodding, doped-out junkie* replied.
Present activity	"Yes," (John) the *jumping man* replied.

When you're stuck for the right way to say it, try . . .

When you've been working and reworking a passage for some time and you still can't figure out how to get it right, try going back to the drawing board and thinking in terms of using a particular grammatical device or trick to get the point across. For example, might your passage read better if you decided to:

Ask a question
Give a command
Introduce a quotation
Change the subject entirely
Simplify
Alter the punctuation
Be funny or tell a joke
Get personal with the reader

56

Turn it into dialogue
Put it in quotes or parentheses
Give examples
Become more emotional
Relate an anecdote
Set it off in a list
Place it under a separate subheading
Box it off
Demonstrate with a drawing, chart, or illustration
Present more facts
Cut it
End it right here

Shift emotional directions in the middle of a sentence.

Sudden emotional changes can be stimulating to readers if done properly. Study the following examples:

"Inside the place smelled pleasantly of freshly baked bread, which was incongruous because everything else was dark and defeated."

"The Moonwalkers were *the* boss, *the* fine group in 1970, *the* flubbed failures, *the* rats in 1975.

" 'I really love you!' she cried, then, 'No—no, I don't. Why did I say that?' "

**Introduce a string of short, descriptive words
and phrases to make an emphatic point.**

A string of terse, hard-hitting sentences loaded with
strong adjectives and images can be highly effective for
injecting a kind of dramatic urgency into your prose.
Note:

> "Oh, I was fat all right. A heavy double. Excellent,
> v-e-r-y rotund. Flaccid and soddy. Pear-bottomed and
> boom-boom-bellied. Sa-sa-sa-sebaceous. A hippopota-
> mus. An eggplant, a trolley car, a smoldering mound.
> Avoirdupois, Incorporated. As big as a lake. As round
> as a school tower. Yehhhhhhh!"

> The dog. Ah, the dog. He'd come touted as being a
> dog. But when he leaped out of the box—yow! A rat!
> A febrile little leaper, this. Complete with rodent-like
> whiskers and twitching, rodent-like nose. Sniff, sniff,
> tremble, tremble. What an odd, unpleasant thing!

Open with a bang; close with an emotion.

The film begins in a Middle Eastern desert where two
archaeologists are digging through an ancient ruin. They
shovel silently for several moments, then one of them
gives an excited shout. Reaching into the sands, he pulls
up a hideous demon mask made entirely of gold. As the
two men stare at each other in wonder, the camera begins

to pan slowly past the diggers, past several large rocks, over to the ruin of a column behind which two sinister men stand watching. One of them slowly lifts a gun and takes aim at the archaeologists, as we DISSOLVE TO. . . .

TV producers call these first minutes of a film the "teaser" and for good reason. This is the segment that is unabashedly designed to keep your eyes tight on the screen and your hands far from the clicker. It's the part that is intended to hook you—and in writing the same formula works equally well: grab your readers as soon as possible, in the first page, in the first paragraph, even in the first word if you can.

How? By using any of the techniques profiled so far: with a mystery, a question, a shocking moment, a conflict, an appeal to a reader's need or emotion, a fast piece of action, an anecdote or humorous story, a brilliant description, a stunning fact, a haunting observation. Whatever it is, make it compelling, make it irresistible, for a thousand things will be competing to gain your reader's attention. The hard truth of the matter is that if you don't win your audience now, right away, you probably won't get them back for a second try.

Then, your ending: Now is the time for resolution and with it an emotional disclosure that sums up your theme. Here is where the deepest meaning of the piece shines through. This is what it's all been about, you see. As in a stage drama, the last impression a literary composition makes should be the strongest as well. "Leave them laughing" is fine; "Leave them moved" is a lot finer.

Avoid unnecessary connectives.

An overabundance of connective words and phrases such as "however," "moreover," "therefore," "furthermore," and "on the other hand," implies that the writer is not skilled enough to move from subject to subject without relying on artificial transitions.

In the following paragraph, the connectives appear in italic type. All can easily be excised without losing a drop of integrity.

"All of Jahangir's reforms were, *in fact,* considered liberal for their day, and *thus* for a time he temporarily became popular with the people. Then, *however,* things started going awry. He persecuted the Jains, drained the treasury, brought the Sikhs to rebellion by executing their leader. He neglected his personal duties and, *moreover,* withdrew to the company of idle fops."

(Thus) when correcting, go on a seek-and-destroy mission for unneeded connectives. (And) when you find ones that are not absolutely essential—(note that) sometimes they will be—expunge them. (Similarly,) if you find yourself using one of these connectives too frequently, especially a "however" or a "furthermore," try to devise a better method of making the crossover. (Again,) you might experiment with different sentence structures and word groupings.

For example, one person writes: "The times were hard

yet they were profitable." Another gives the construction a creative parallelism: "The times were hard; the times were profitable."

One person writes: "The pendulum swung freely. Therefore, Fritz concluded, the weights are the same." Another eliminates the connective and makes the scene more dramatic: "The pendulum swung freely. Aha! The weights are the same, thought Fritz."

One person writes: "Altogether, we all must now assume that the evidence is undeniable." Another loses the "altogether" and substitutes a tighter phrase in its place: "The evidence, it now seems clear to all of us, is undeniable."

Don't weaken your prose with too many adverbial qualifiers.

"Usually," "probably," "ordinarily," "mostly," "mainly," "generally," "as a rule"—all such weakly explanatory adverbs and adverbial phrases have their place in clear writing. But not when tossed in simply to cover an author's scholarly tracks. The frightened writer in such cases is, you see, buying a little insurance, just in case some voice of authority comes along later to announce that "not *every* robin's egg is blue" or "Le Roux didn't *always* mix his own paints."

Well and good. By qualifying several times that *most* robin's eggs are blue and that Le Roux *usually* mixed paints himself, all exceptions are provided for and all bets hedged. The problem is that the writer appears wordy and pedantic in the process, for he or she has sacrificed style and rhythm on the altar of compulsive accuracy.

Worse too, the impression such writing produces sometimes ends up causing its opposite effect, making readers feel that the author is overcautious, not for accuracy's sake but out of ignorance.

In many cases details must be qualified, especially in technical and medical writing. On the other hand, especially if you're working on scholarly prose, be on guard. Go over your work with an editor's eye and remove all unnecessary, play-it-safe qualifiers that bog down the forward momentum of your writing.

Use intentional redundancy on occasion.

A fun trick that can produce excellent and sometimes unexpected effects is the intentional repetition of similar words or sounds. A poignant example is this bit of graffiti found scrawled on a military vehicle in Vietnam: "We are the unwilling, led by the unqualified, doing the unnecessary, for the ungrateful." An interesting subliminal side effect of this verse, unintentional perhaps, but subtly dominant, is that "un" rhymes with "gun."

Here's another.

"No, I would not bow. No, I would not scrape. No, I would not empty the wash bowl. No, I would not sweep the vestibule. No, I would not carry the water bucket on my head. No, I would not chop the master's wood. No, I

would not serve. No, no, and again no—because I am not
a slave."

**Make your sentences rise to a climax: let
them reveal their most significant
information at the end.**

Save the best for last. This holds true for individual
sentences as well as for entire stories.

Try it. Start low, increase the intensity as you go, then
reveal the denouement at the end of the sentence. Examples:

> "Only one more indispensable massacre of Capital-
> ists or Communists or Fascists or Christians or Here-
> tics, and there we are—there we are, in the golden
> future.
>
> —ALDOUS HUXLEY

> "A sign of celebrity is that a man's name is worth
> more than his service."
>
> —DANIEL BOORSTIN

> "As a general, I beat the Austrians in battle simply
> because they did not know the importance of five min-
> utes."
>
> —NAPOLEON BONAPARTE

> "What causes the discrepancy between the gratitude
> we receive and the gratitude we expect is that the pride

of the giver and the pride of the taker cannot agree on the value of the gift."

—DE LA ROCHEFOUCAULD

"Our real voyage of discovery consists not in seeking new landscape but in having new eyes."

—MARCEL PROUST

"All poets want you to write poetry just like their own—only worse."

—ANONYMOUS

"Too smart is dumb."

—GERMAN PROVERB

Use grace notes.

A grace note is a gratuitous aside or action that adds unexpected humor and/or emotional color to your writing. Grace notes often appear in film scripts. In the movie *Crocodile Dundee II,* for instance, the hero, Dundee, is cooking an egg and drops it on the floor. A detective who brazenly invites himself to breakfast is then served the egg and proceeds to pick small pieces of grit out of his teeth as he talks vociferously about a murder plot. This subtle bit of comic relief is beautifully underplayed. The detective never refers to the grit, nor is there further mention of the event. Yet the counterpoint between the humorous sight gag and the serious lines which the detective delivers as he eats makes the grit-in-the-eggs bit truly entertaining business.

The same device can be used with equal power in compositional writing. The grace notes in the following examples are italicized:

"Finally, Thomas Aquinas attempted to uplift the human spirit with his writing and to bring peace and wisdom to the entire Catholic world. His spirit remains on earth today. His greatness lives. *Onward and upward.*"

"Turn the crepes over lightly and start the brown rice. Be sure you have cleaned the rice thoroughly, as natural brown rice sometimes has stones in it. (*Ouch! There goes a bicuspid!*)"

"The cavalry literally arrived in the last five minutes with guns blazing to save Fort Abernathe (*complete with a general whose picture today looks amazingly like John Wayne*). But it was not soon enough to save the lives of a dozen farmers who were caught outside the fort's gate."

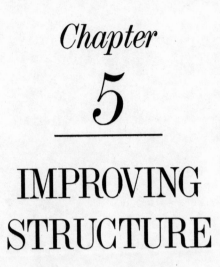

Chapter 5

IMPROVING STRUCTURE

STRUCTURE—the total form and organization of a literary composition—is determined by the relationships established between theme, action, exposition, narrative, imagery, tone, and style. If a composition is tight, well organized, and logically presented; if it contains no loose ends and unresolved conflicts; if its pace, mode of expression, and point of view are harmoniously integrated, then we say its structure is unified. If not, then not. Ye shall know a poor literary structure by the sum of its ill-fitting parts.

When writing non-fiction, move from the general to the specific.

Start off with a general statement of fact, then methodically fill in the significant points one by one, starting with the most important and moving down the priority scale to the last, most trivial detail. The end of the piece then sums up the main point of view and adds an interesting observation or two to tie the whole composition together.

This practical approach to factual writing can be boiled down to a formula, oversimplified perhaps, but germane:

1. Lead with your main idea, or thesis.
2. Give a few examples.
3. Restate your thesis, this time enlarging on it.
4. Give more specific examples and more detail.
5. Make your final points, reach a conclusion, and end with a final message or observation.

The following article does all this with concision and expertise:

Twenty years ago vagabond men and women living in parks and subway tunnels were an unusual sight in our major cities. Today they have become as much a part of the urban landscape as trucks and pigeons. In New York City alone over 40,000 persons are without permanent shelter. Los Angeles has almost as many. In several major cities homelessness is increasing at the rate of more than 10 percent a year. What's behind it all?

A number of factors, it seems, all of which have come home to roost in the 1980's. For one, government cutbacks in health care during the past decade have caused previously institutionalized mentally ill patients to be released onto the streets. The recent upsurge in urban drug abuse, mainly crack-oriented, has likewise impoverished hundreds-of-thousands of persons and left them with no place to go but the parks and subways. In cities the sharp increase in rents, cutbacks in Welfare, lack of adequate housing, reduction of SRO hotels, abandonment of rent control, and the impoverishment caused by inflation have all contributed to a derelict population. So have unemployment in ghettos, massive migrations of illegal aliens, and the slowdown in the construction of public housing. And, of course, there is the ever-present specter of urban over-population—if the truth be told, many American cities simply have too many people and not enough places to put them.

In short, the homeless phenomenon is a sign of our times, a modern urban catastrophe with political, social, psychological, and spiritual causes that extend far back into time. What can be done to help? Shelters are a temporary answer, but these dig deep into the pockets of the already staggering tax payer. Drug rehabilitation programs will help, as will an increase in government subsidies for housing and health care. Of all things, however, better employment opportunities, improved quality of education, and an across-the-board relief from sociological stresses and pressures are all necessary. In the long run, an adjusted, healthy, educated person who holds a good job is far less likely to take to the streets than one who looks into the past—and the future—and sees nothing but rejection and desperation. Only sound persons make a sound society.

Plant questions as you go along.

Plant little queries along the way, little hints and teasers. Then answer them one by one, substituting new queries as you do. For example:

> "Louis's army remained faithful during the first days of the siege. But the nettlesome question still remained: In time of attack who would guard the guards?"

> "Freud's private chambers were almost never available for private consultation, Lawrence learned, and only once was a patient allowed inside. Who was this privileged patient? Lawrence wondered. He turned to several of Freud's private correspondences to find out."

> "All the flames coming from the potassium jets were blue but the next to last. The very jet Professor Rick had ignored. 'Curious,' thought Bluntvale. 'Very curious.' "

Make frequent promises that excitement or insight will soon be revealed to the reader.

Sometimes an entire story can be made to turn on a single promise of things to come. In *Treasure Island* we are kept reading both by the tantalizing premise of buried treasure and the fact that *somebody's going to find it.* Will it be the pirates or Jim Hawkins's band?

In *Jane Eyre* the author hints in several different ways that Rochester, the moody hero, has a mysterious guest living in his attic and that this guest represents the key to his strange behavior. We keep reading to find out who he/she/it is.

You can make an enticing promise in a line or two. For example:

> "I looked Mat straight in the eyes. I knew we'd meet again—soon."

> "Hitler's tank battalion was stalled for the moment on the left flank near Addis. But Rommel, as always, had something deadly up his sleeve."

> "Forget calorie counting—it's too slow and difficult. Forget crash diets—they damage your health. Forget the special "medical" diets—some work, some don't. If you go with any of these regimes your chances of keeping weight off permanently are 50 to 1, and that's a scientifically proven fact. Don't worry though: there *are* methods that will take fat off and keep it off. Want to know which one is the best?"

Always include some type of conflict.

It's a not-so-well-kept secret among writers that the principle of conflict and resolution, so dear to the novelist's heart, applies just as successfully to exposition and nonfiction as it does to fiction, even the most theoretical and academic kinds.

This does not mean that you should introduce a heroine in distress into an essay on dairy farming or bookbinding, only that a conflicted situation of *some* kind, be it an unexpected case of hoof-and-mouth disease or a poorly mended book cover, will keep interest level high. Remember, conflict does not necessarily result from an argument or warlike confrontation. It can come, both in life and in literature, from relatively unexpected and quiet places, such as:

A fallacy

A situation that needs improvement

A challenge

A political, social, psychological, or personal disagreement

A mystery or enigma

An insoluble dilemma

An emotional or psychological quandary

A theoretical or scientific disagreement

A person in trouble

A sudden shock or change

A small misunderstanding that escalates

If you are writing a science report on gravity, say, first set the stage: Newton was faced with a conflict: What, he wondered, caused objects to fall *down* rather than *up?*

If you are writing a biography, make sure that one protagonist—a nasty parent, an unfaithful spouse, a suppressive boss—is given plenty of play. Then show how the main character copes with it all.

If you are writing a letter to a business associate requesting aid or increased funds, first clearly depict the conflict: our stamping machines are outmoded, and if they are not replaced soon we will fall behind the competition. Our telecommunications system is too small for the office; we are losing important incoming calls every day.

When you're stuck for an ending, go back to your beginning.

When stymied for a way to end your piece, go back to the first line, the first paragraph, the first page, the first chapter, and reread it several times. Since opposites tend to meet in some mysterious way, you will often discover that the ending is somehow logically implied in the beginning and that your very first ideas somehow also contain a logical conclusion.

Whenever possible, tell a story.

Because most minds are captivated by narrative action, because most of us cut our molars on fairy tales and adventure yarns, and because somehow the story form itself makes reading more interesting ("In art, truth that is boring is not true," Isaac Bashevis Singer once remarked), astute writers try to give the structure of their work some type of narrative thrust. This includes nonfiction as well as fiction; the story motif works just as nicely with writing advertising copy, a school essay, even a report on a cooking class.

Let's imagine the dullest scenario we can think of and see how it might be made interesting by the use of story. Suppose, let's say, you are penning an essay on the working of the electric milk separator, the device that separates cream from milk.

Zzzzzzzzz! Snore! But wait, remember the writer's axiom: every subject, every situation, every scene contains *some* potential drama. Or phrased differently: there is no subject or situation that cannot be *turned into* a story.

How? Start by reviewing all your information. Look for hidden conflict or tension. Ask yourself:

- What is the potential for action here? For excitement and diversion?

- What is the most inherently interesting thing about this subject?

- In what ways might I create narrative interest by appealing to the reader's five senses?

- Is there any change or transformation that takes place in the subject?

- Is there inherent danger or conflict?

- Is there anything about this material that can be used to fascinate my audience? Horrify them?

Amaze them? Is there an inherent struggle implied? An unanswered question? Something inspirational? Something anecdotal or potentially humorous? Is there some way I can bring the reader directly into the situation?

As it turns out, the method by which milk is separated from cream lends itself to several narrative possibilities, namely, appealing to the senses, dramatizing change and transformation, and bringing the reader into the action. In this case the writer decides to use all three to turn his piece into a you-are-there experience. The final literary result is, if not Balzacian, enough to keep most people reading:

Now we've arrived at the cream extraction quarters. Notice that massive, gleaming steel tank in the center of the room? It's silent now. But in a moment a tall man with a white uniform will walk by and throw a small switch. Then watch as literally thousands of gallons of billowy milk come shooting out from hidden gaskets in the ceiling. Watch as the tank fills with milk, then begins to rotate on its pins like a gigantic mixing bowl. Slowly at first, then faster and faster, until it moves at propeller-like speeds and the milk inside is formed into a whirling white maelstrom.

Now look into the center of the bowl. Some of the liquid is congealing into a putty-like substance and is draining down in spirals through a run-off funnel, into a stainless steel barrel below. This is the end product, the cream, the prize, the thick, white essence. From begin-

ning to end the whole operation has been curiously sen-
suous and appetizing, and, in fact, you can now run your
finger over the top edge of the barrel, scrape off a bit
of the rich cream, and enjoy a momentary holiday in
Devonshire.

There are, in other words, many possible dramatic
vignettes hidden in almost anything you might imagine.
The challenge—and the fun—is in finding them.

Let each paragraph become a ministory unto itself.

A story element can also be implanted into paragraphs
and even individual sentences. "A dramatic necessity goes
deep into the nature of the sentence," writes Robert Frost.
"Sentences are not different enough to hold the attention
unless they are dramatic. No ingenuity of varying structure will do." Look, for example, at this palindrome (a
sentence that reads the same forward and backward):
"A man, a plan, a canal: Panama." Some anonymous
word artist has sketched the story of the building of the
Panama Canal in seven simple words, an amazing feat
when you think about it. An even more evocative example is this:

"Hey, Who was dat lady I seen you with last night?"
"Dat was no lady, dat was my wife."

In two sentences the author of this classic put-down has shown us a marriage in a nutshell, a cautionary tale complete with characterization and psychological interaction. In one quick moment of recognition we picture the man who is asking the question. He is clearly uneducated, a "dees, dems, and dose" type, a friendly fellow, probably, though not a particularly close friend of the person he is talking to; otherwise he would recognize the man's wife. Chances are, in fact, that these two men know each other only casually, perhaps from occasional meetings at Frankie's Bar and Grill, say, or from studying the racing sheets together at the track.

The second man, the one who answers the question, presents us with further humorous but poignant impressions. We sense the acrimony that has long festered between him and his wife, the years of name-calling, the middle-of-the-night bag-packing sessions and divorce threats. His wife is probably *not* a lady either, when all is said and done, a fact that her husband is most anxious to tell almost anyone—thus making him, *ipso facto*, not a gentleman.

Ultimately we imagine these two poor souls holing up in a low-rent tenement somewhere, a dingy room straight out of the *Honeymooners*. They are just now arguing over who used up the last of the ketchup, or which TV shows to watch tonight. As they bicker we can picture the faces of their friends and the long-suffering whines of their beleaguered children. An entire past, present and future come clear—all this in two quick sentences.

A plotting game to get you started:

When you're stuck for ideas about what to write about—this particularly applies to fiction writers—try your luck at pulling your outline out of a hat.

Take a piece of paper and write down the following eight headings:

The Hero
The Heroine
The Enemy
The Place
The Obstacles
The Predicaments
The Climax
The Resolution

Under the first heading prepare a list of 25 possible personas for your hero, numbering each as you go.

For instance, your hero might be a (1) pro football player (2) spy (3) rock singer (4) heart surgeon (5) acrobat (6) literary agent (7) commando (8) Vietnam vet (9) cowboy (10) reformed thief (11) modern-day explorer (12) student (13) detective (14) circus performer (15) movie star (16) brilliant dropout professor (17) atomic scientist (18) ex–drug addict (19) bum (20) commercial pilot (21) psychiatrist (22) cub reporter (23) classical violinist (24) appliance salesman (25) president of a Fortune 500 company.

Under the second heading do the same for your heroine. She can be a (1) nurse (2) head of a small pharmaceuticals company (3) owner of a restaurant (4) writer (5) bartender (6) cowgirl (7) stripper (8) advertising executive (9) refugee from a Russian concentration camp (10) actress (11) secretary at a large accounting firm (12) millionaire's daughter (13) history scholar (14) gypsy (15) call girl (16) debutante (17) magician's helper (18) housewife (19) school principal (20) short-order cook (21) bicycle messenger (22) cripple (23) French governess (24) disc jockey (25) interior decorator.

Make up similar entries under the remaining six categories. Typical Enemies might include an undercover spy, a false friend, a cruel boss, a dictator, a drug czar, a spurned lover, a person who secretly seeks revenge, a serial killer, a jealous rival.

For Place you might use a hospital, a farm, high in the Andes Mountains, the Gobi desert, a large office complex, a mythical kingdom, the military, a professional athletic facility, a dance studio.

For Obstacles there's the likes of lack of money, a stern parent, a mean boss, an unclimbable peak, an unbridgeable social barrier, the threat of war, opposing sides in a legal battle, or a serious disease.

For Predicaments you might opt for one of these: the hero is illegally detained, someone loses all their money, an armed rebellion breaks out, someone loses their arm in an accident, a person is fired from a job, a contract exists that cannot be broken, a person is hopelessly addicted, a person has a child who requires constant medical care.

For Climax imagine situations such as these: a fire destroys all, a character threatens suicide, an entire fortune is placed at risk, a dangerous mission is undertaken, the imprisonment of an important person becomes imminent, a bad accident occurs, a secret enemy emerges, a hidden benefactor makes himself or herself known.

For Resolution: the enemy is caught in a trap, the rivals are bested, someone confesses, the whole thing turns out to be a con, the enemy's plan backfires and destroys him or her, the person we thought was an enemy turns out to be a friend, an escape takes place, a disguise is revealed, someone now sees things clearly.

Once you have thought up all twenty-five variables for each heading, write down the numbers 1 through 25 on a piece of paper and cut them out.

Next, spread out your headings and variables in front of you. Now starts the fun. Take the numbers, put them in a hat (or whatever), and draw eight at random.

Under each heading write down the item that corresponds to the number. If the first number you draw is 6, look up the sixth item under the first heading: it is "a literary agent." If your second number is 2, your heroine is "the head of a small pharmaceuticals company." Do the same for the rest of the headings. Your completed list may resemble the following table:

Heading	Variable
HERO	A literary agent
HEROINE	Head of a pharmaceuticals company

ENEMY	A spurned lover
PLACE	A military instillation
OBSTACLES	An unbridgeable social barrier
PREDICAMENTS	A contract exists that cannot be broken
CLIMAX	A dangerous mission is undertaken
RESOLUTION	The person we thought was the enemy turns out to be a friend

You now have the outline of a potential story in your hands. Your main characters are established, as is your place, climax, and resolution. Study the sequence as a unity and let your creative imagination fill in the gaps. With a bit of figuring you should be able to develop a logical plot from what's before you. If two variables cannot be made to mesh, or if you don't like a particular combination, draw another number or two and change it. It's all just a game, naturally, but an interesting one, and one which may trigger who-knows-what bright ideas.

Always know where you're going.

Although some writers, especially fiction writers, improvise as they go along, most seasoned pros will assure you that it's ultimately more expedient to know in advance how you are going to structure your piece.

This means: know your beginning, know your end, know your facts. Know what style and tone you wish to effect. Know your theme, your message, your point of view. Perhaps most importantly, know why you are writing this piece in the first place, who you are writing it for, and what you really wish to say.

It is no doubt glib to assert that once you have all this information at your fingertips the rest of the composition will fall into place. But—most likely it will.

Chapter

6

CORRECTING, REWRITING, AND SURVIVING

O NCE your main piece is written the real work now begins: rewriting and correcting. Here, as in all other areas of the writer's game, there are tricks that will make the task easier. Note:

Don't attempt serious rewriting when you're tired or in a bad mood.

While it's ultimately a matter of taste and experience, you will find that many writers, most perhaps, *reread* their material in the evening, making small corrections here and there as they go, then *rewrite* the next day, usually in the morning.

Why? Because after 5 or 6 P.M. the eagerness and pep of the day's beginnings give way to the lassitude and mellowness of evening. Intuition works more slowly, and the eye takes longer to move across the printed page. We tend to be picky, faultfinding, finicky. Now is the time for dotting i's and correcting details, but *not* for massive rewrites. Leave these for the next morning when your critical faculties are counterbalanced by the energy of a new day. By then ten or twelve hours have elapsed. You've had time to think about your work, ponder it, play with it, dream on it. This helps.

The same is true for bad moods. When you're feeling blue, the whole world—including creative efforts—looks blue as well. Judgment becomes accordingly skewed, and you end up crossing out passages that on a brighter day might seem inspired. The fact is that our psychological and physiological states do affect our creative decisions, and if we are going to maximize our rewriting time, it's best to do it when we're feeling rested, alert, and optimistic.

Warm up by rewriting.

An excellent way to start writing for the day is to review work from yesterday and spend a few minutes rewriting it. This will focus you, help circulate your mental juices, and get you reinvolved in past trains of thought. Once the engine is purring, *then* switch over to original stuff.

Put it away for a day . . . week . . . month . . . year.

Is it a writer's axiom? Probably. It goes like this: The more time you allow between writing, rewriting, and rereading, the more objective you will be about what you've written. Here's the recipe—and schedule—I recommend:

- When writing any report or work of nonfiction: Do *not* reread it the next day. Wait at least three days. A week is better if you have the time, and two weeks better still. Then reread and correct.

- When writing a short story: Wait at least a month before rereading it and rewriting it.

- When writing a novel: Finish it, correct it, rewrite it, re-rewrite it, and put it away for six months. (An entire year would buy you even more objectivity, but that's asking a lot.) Then take it down, read, and revise as required.

Never submit a first draft.

It is said that many of Alexandre Dumas's early novels, before he started hiring stables of authors to write for him, were penned in a single, uncorrected draft. The master, eyewitnesses report, spewed his stories out in several prolonged sittings without so much as a quick reread afterward, then gave his massive piles of parchment over to his publisher. Perhaps.

First-draft manuscripts are fine if you are a genius, of course, or unavoidable if you are short on time. Otherwise: revise, revise, revise. Hemingway said that good writing is 10 percent inspiration, 90 percent perspiration. The perspiration comes in the going-over, in the rereading, the rethinking, the rephrasing, the retrying, the redoing, the rewriting—re, re, re. Don't stint on it. If it doesn't click, there's usually a reason. Probably it needs more work. Trust your instincts. Go back to the writing board and keep working, keep revising, keep correcting, until you're sure.

Get several intelligent readings before you submit your work.

After your manuscript is complete, or even if you're in the middle, outside feedback helps. Now is the time to find several persons whose advice you respect. Give them your manuscript plus your full permission to return an honest appraisal. Then, most important of all, prepare for the possible flak that will follow. Be ready for off-the-wall comments, for points missed, and remarkably wrong interpretations. But be prepared as well for incisive comments that cut to the heart of the matter—and to yours as well. For criticism can hurt, especially when it's accurate. At any rate, hear what's said and think about it. If the shoe fits, make the necessary changes. If not, forget about it and go on.

Three similar criticisms make a quorum.

Everyone who reads your work will have *something* to say about it. One person raves, the next is indifferent. A third thinks it "needs work." A fourth tells you, "Very sorry, but it just sort of sticks in my throat" (to which you might answer, as Eudora Welty once did: "But darling, you were supposed to read it, not eat it!").

Fine. That's horse racing. Do pay attention, however, when several persons, let's say three minimum, go over your offering and all come up with the same criticisms.

The rule of thumb here is: When several readers whose opinions you respect come to similar negative conclusions, there's almost sure to be some truth at the bottom of their criticisms. After a certain point it can no longer be counted as coincidence. Revisions are in order.

Read what you've written out loud.

A simple, tried-and-true trick. Read your work aloud to yourself or have someone else read it to you. Then judge. Hearing is different from reading, and you will catch many subtle errors in tone, rhythm, and phrasing that you might otherwise miss.

Another technique is to read your day's work into a tape recorder and play it back. Same idea, same results.

Write in all your corrections clearly.

This sounds almost stupid in its obviousness. Like reminding a writer to dot his or her i's. And yet, and yet—how many times have we had difficulty rereading our own penned revisions? How many pages of astute corrections have we lost to the demon of poor penmanship?

The trick is simply to put the brakes on when your script passes the legibility barrier and when your words begin to look like cuneiform markings. Remind yourself what a pain it was in the past to find precious notes and corrections unreadable. Then—consciously—make an effort to revise in a slower, tidier way. You'll thank yourself a lot for this one later on.

A tip for estimating words per page:

Editors often speak of a book's length in number of words rather than in pages. This is a confusing prospect to many writers, though it doesn't have to be. Word count is easily determined by a four-step formula:

1. Count the number of words on five typically sized pages and add them all up.
2. Divide the total word count by 5 pages to find the average number of words per page.
3. Multiply this average by the number of pages in your manuscript.
4. Round off the total to the nearest 100 words.

Let's say you have a manuscript of 300 pages. Take five typically sized pages from the stack and count the words on each.

You will get, let's say, 299, 317, 331, 289, and 301 words per page. Add them up. The total is 1537 words.

Now divide 1537 words by 5 pages. The answer is 307.4 which, rounded off, makes 307 words per page on average.

Finally, multiply 307 by 300, your number of manuscript pages. Your manuscript is approximately 92,100 words in length.

Let your first draft run long.

Don't edit yourself on the first draft; don't let the fear of overwriting stop you from letting fly. You probably will overwrite, but so what? You'll be cutting pages soon enough. The idea at this point is simply to get it all down, to say what you want to say and to include everything you want to include. If your piece is supposed to run five pages, let it go seven or eight. Or ten. Don't be afraid; no one is watching, no one is criticizing. After you have indulged yourself by getting it all on paper, turn the discipline machine on and take out extraneous words and passages. When the time comes to revise, remember:

When in doubt, cut.

I once told a writer friend of mine that I was worried about my latest project. "Why?" he asked. "Because," I said, "My editor asked me to cut almost a fifth of it."

He looked at me for a moment, then got an odd smile on his face. "Good" was all he said.

And he was right. It's good to cut.

Why? Because trim and lean reads better than wordy and ponderous. It just does. Because nothing clogs style more than excess words, extraneous details, cliches, jargon, the same ideas repeated over and over again in slightly different phrasing. Remember, others will never see what's lying on your cutting room floor. They will never know about those brilliant, unnecessary passages mildewing in the wastebasket. And what they don't know won't hurt them—or you.

To cut or not to cut, therefore, is really not the question. If you have to ask, if the possibility of removing a certain passage has already come up, that's usually proof that it should go. Some voice inside is telling you something. Listen to it; act on it. If you can't decide, give the piece to someone else for a reading, get their advice— then cut it anyway. When in doubt, cut.

When your manuscript is completed, try cutting your first page.

Go ahead, try it. The whole thing. Or if that doesn't work, part of it. Most writers tend to be at their worst in the first few pages. It's stage fright, mostly, coupled with overeagerness and the tendency to put in unnecessary details. Later on when they read what they've written they're amazed to discover how many of these early para-

graphs are freighted with ponderous introductory re-
marks and needless facts. "Did I really write all that?"

See how much of the first page is whittle-able material.
Even a paragraph's removal can help, and sometimes even
a teeny-weeny bit taken from the second page doesn't
hurt. You'll be surprised.

Hints for efficient cutting.

When you cut, think of two things: tightening up and
taking out. Sometimes what you've written is just not up
to snuff; it must go. Sometimes, on the other hand, the
material is basically fine. It simply needs pruning and
reshuffling. Be careful to make this important distinction; don't throw out the baby with the bath water.

What's more, certain stylistic and grammatical elements naturally tend to attract deadwood and lend themselves easily to scissors. The following are all examples:

1. *Unnecessary adverbs*   Much prose, even good prose,
abounds in these: "very," "some," "quite," "any." Removing the ones that are not *absolutely* necessary tightens up
style. Say "it was hot," not "it was quite hot." Say "I
carried food with me." not "I carried some food with me."
Say "I hope," not "I only hope." Say "it was rude of him,"
not "it was somewhat rude of him."

2. *Unnecessary adjectives*   While we are dutifully
warned in writing class to use strong nouns and verbs and
to go easy on the adjectives, adjectives remain the ice
cream and cake of prose and are irresistible even to the

best of writers. Avoid temptation if you can—or at least be moderate about giving in to it—and if you can't, make up for it later by cutting. A good way to do this is to read your sentence over *with* the adjective and *without,* see if the sentence is weakened by removing it, then follow Thoreau's advice: "As to the adjective: when in doubt, strike it out."

3. Phrases that can be compressed   Shorten "deity figure" to "deity." Change "academic line of college subjects" to "courses." Let "nighttime" become "night." Cut "whatever thing you want" to "whatever you want."

4. Wordy lines   The sentence "I was born in the city of Cleveland, which is in Ohio" can be cut down to "I was born in Cleveland, Ohio." The statement, "All sincere students should strive very hard to achieve improved grades" can be trimmed to "Sincere students should strive to improve their grades."

5. Overly long introductory and rhetorical phrases George Orwell says it as well as it has ever been said:

> Phrases like *not unjustifiable assumption, leaves much to be desired, would serve no good purpose, a consideration which we should do well to bear in mind,* are a continuous temptation, a packet of aspirins always at one's elbow. . . . This invasion of one's mind by ready-made phrases (*lay the foundations, achieve a radical transformation*), can only be prevented if one is constantly on guard against them, and every such phrase anesthetizes a portion of one's brain.

6. Unnecessary sentences   Most of us have a tendency in first-draft writing to repeat ourselves. Read over what you've written carefully, looking for redundant lines and needless rephrasings.

7. *Unnecessary clauses* "The picture of the boy who is dressed in green" can be pruned to "the picture of the boy in green." "The amusement park, which is located in Virginia Beach, is open to all" can be reduced to the "The amusement park in Virginia Beach is open to all."

Save all rewritten and corrected materials.

Don't throw away *anything* you've written until your manuscript is completed. All removed passages, all rewritten pages, should be filed in a folder or kept on disk for possible further use. Later on you may want to return a cut section to your manuscript, and you'll be thankful that you didn't chuck it. Or you may want to use what you've written today for a project in the future. Your excised materials are a valuable record and resource. Save them.

If you feel it's right, it probably is.

Trust your inner voice. If a passage satisfies you, it probably will satisfy others as well. If something seems vaguely ajar, if you're not entirely comfortable with the sound and sense of it, others are likely to have the same reaction. Trust your feelings, trust your intuition.

But if you still feel it's wrong:

Often, of course, it's difficult to be precise about what's wrong. You just *feel* it's not what you want to say. Good. This is instinct at work. The best thing to do when such doubts nag is to put your work away for a while and reread it later, asking yourself the hard questions:

- Is my tone right? Am I approaching the subject with the proper respect? Humor? Emotion? Facts?

- Am I being too wordy? Am I repeating myself? Am I taking too long to say what I have to say? Or, does my piece need fleshing out?

- Are all my facts accurate? Is my research persuasive and thorough? Have I omitted important points?

- Are my characters (or characterizations) believable? Are my ideas credible? Do I argue my point with clarity, logic, and precision? Do I sound persuasive?

- Is my choice of vocabulary appropriate in the given context? Do I rely too much on cliches or hackneyed phrases? Conversely, does my attempt to write in an original way sound pretentious?

- Do my sentences flow naturally one into the other? Do they move from idea to idea without leaving gaps or making jumps?

- Do my paragraphs blend together into a coherent whole? Is there continuity from the beginning of the piece to the end?

- Do the transitions between paragraphs flow naturally? Do I use connectives well? Do I use too many of them? Too few?

- Are time sequences clearly spelled out? Are all events recorded in their proper order? Is there confusion about who's doing what, when?

- Are my grammar and usage correct? How about spelling and punctuation? Do all pronouns agree? Any dangling modifiers?

- Is the rhythm satisfying? Do the words sound right when I read them? Do they flow pleasingly?

- Are my sentences crafted to produce their maximum intellectual and/or emotional effect? Which ones, if any, can be improved?

- Have I left any dramatic, intellectual, or emotional questions unanswered, any strings untied? Are all thematic issues clarified and concluded?

After testing yourself against these queries and making any appropriate rewrites, go over the passages again. Do they sound better now? Do they *feel* better? Whatever you do, don't hand in your work until you believe in it.

Stop writing for the day when you're ahead.

By any standards, the discipline of writing is a difficult one, and any carrot you can dangle to keep yourself returning with enthusiasm is worth a lot. For instance, some writers quit for the day in the middle of a well flowing passage, knowing that tomorrow they will be able to pick up at an interesting and manageable spot. Others shut down the typewriter when they get a good idea. They jot it down and let it percolate in their brains until the following day. Still others stop for work when they are feeling challenged by a particular passage—the prospect of figuring out what to do next keeps them coming back for more. Similar tricks that will help in this regard include:

Leave yourself notes.

Before calling it a day, some writers jot down notes to themselves for tomorrow's work. For instance:

> *Note:* I stopped at the section on asthma medicine profiles. I have described Isoetharine and Metaproterenol so far. Tomorrow I will pick up with Terbutaline and Albuterol. Remember to include a diagram of a metered dose inhaler. See Johnson's *Inhalers,* pages 42–45 for details. Other sections to include in this chapter: chart of beta-adrenergic bronchodilators; preventive medications (Cromolyn sodium); and corticosteroids.

Such a record can help you stay organized from one day's writing session to the next. No need to get compulsive about it, of course. Some writers jot down short outlines or topic ideas which they then leave on top of the typewriter for later inspection. Others write only three or four key ideas on file cards, then place them into a box specially marked "Today's Subjects." The first thing they do when sitting down next morning is to go through the box and use the ideas as a point of departure.

Keep notebooks.

For any writer, the events of the day bring some measure of fresh experience: overheard conversations, interesting characters and confrontations, emotional highs and lows—all of which are grist for the writing mill. Even a single unusual encounter can trigger a rush of ideas that leads to creative breakthroughs. "Ideas tend to travel in flocks," as Marjorie Holmes puts it.

But, as you've also noticed, the mind is not a foolproof retainer of such impressions; the sad truth is that unless they are written down quickly they sift away like sand.

Notebooks are the answer. Keep several of them; most writers do. They can be pocket-sized, spiral variety, or even three-hole binders, depending on whether you use them in the field or at your desk. Keep a small one in your pocket or purse, along with a pen. Have a notebook by your bedside for night thoughts and another near your workplace for inspirations.

Depending on the kind of writing you do, any of the following subjects are worthy of a notebook, or at least of a section within one:

Dialogue and conversation notebook   Record significant passages from overheard conversations. Keep note of verbal exchanges you overhear in barber shops, powder rooms, bowling alleys, bars, beauty salons, elevators, locker rooms, church socials, supermarkets, department stores, conference rooms, taxis, buses, planes. Document colorful accents. Jot down interesting word usage and regional twists of phrase.

Insights, story ideas, phrases, observations   These will visit you at the oddest times. My moments of inspiration tend to come in the bathtub or when I'm falling asleep at night. I try to arrange it so that a notebook is within fetching distance when they do. Experience has taught me that like dreams, no matter how vivid an idea may seem when it occurs, it fades from memory within hours and sometimes within minutes.

Interesting vocabulary words   When you come upon a strange or eloquent or ridiculous word, jot it down. Recent additions to my collection include these nifty improbabilities:

Heresiarch   The founder or chief protagonist of a heresy

Stochastic   Characteristic of conjecture; involving the chance of probability

Midden   A dung hill or refuse heap, especially one left in a primitive habitation

Uncinate   Having a hooked end

Such words are the rare butterflies of the language: I pin them into the leaves of my notebooks; I pore over them at night like a collector. I will use only a fraction of these lexigraphic oddities in my work, of course. The point is, coming into contact with a wide range of words makes our feeling for the language that much bolder and broader. Words are the tools of our trade. We must treasure them.

Facts and statistics   Surprising, controversial, intriguing facts make any piece of writing glow. When you hear one or read one or are told one, jot it down and place it on file. Keep track of noteworthy items you find in newspapers, books, films, radio, TV, magazines, encyclopedias, almanacs. Some writers make their livings solely by producing volumes full of odd information tidbits.

Newspaper clippings   An agent once told me that a writer should be able to come up with at least three good book or magazine ideas every morning simply from reading the daily paper. She's right. If one has eyes to see, the dailies are crammed with marketable stories, both fiction and nonfiction, commercial and academic. Headline ideas that triggered magazine or book notions for me this week include:

"The Dark Side of Medical Care"
"Pollution Spoiled It All: Why Tyrone Nevins Had to Leave His Home on the Bulleh River"

"Traces of an Ancient Undersea Mine Found in Bahamas"
"Large Numbers of Derelicts Said To Be Living in the Tunnels of Penn Station"

You get the picture. Though the reportage itself may not be useful, a single idea lurking within it can trigger a plot, an article line, a screenplay, a dramatic character, whatever. George Antonich, the detective story writer, once told of reading a newspaper item about a man whose clothes caught on fire and who drowned trying to put them out when he jumped into a barrel of water. Pondering this odd event, Antonich let his imagination craft an entire short story based on suicide and insurance payments. Later on he sold the story to *Alfred Hitchcock's Mystery Magazine* for a sizeable sum.

Bibliographies Whenever you find a book of value, record its title, the author's name, publisher, and date. Annotate each entry with a line or two saying what the book is about and how it might be of value. If it's a library book, make note of its call number. My own bibliographical journal is composed of

1. Books I have used in the past on specific projects
2. Books I think will be of value in projects to come
3. Books in the specific fields I write about
4. Books of general interest

Interesting, witty, and significant quotations As a writer I constantly comb anthologies for sayings that have punch and pith. I jot them down in my notebook, and above each quotation I write the subject(s) to which it pertains. Later on I will use these phrases to add zest and authority to my own prose.

For example, in my notebook today I recorded an insightful statement from Albert Camus: "The future is the only kind of property that the masters willingly concede to the slaves." Interesting. Worth saving. So I write it down and over this entry in bold letters I pen, "THE FUTURE," and also "TYRANNY," "SLAVERY," and finally "TOTALITARIANISM." Next time I need a quote on any of these subjects I will have it on hand.

Tricks for working through writer's block:

Sometimes the words don't come, those demon words. Zip. No matter how hard you push, the boulder that seals your creativity continues to roll back, Sisyphus-like.

Every writer has remedies for this perennial dilemma. My own, several of which I learned from other writers, include diversion, relaxation, and physical activity.

Let's go over them one at a time:

1. Diversion Just stop. Simple as that. Remove yourself; keep a safe distance from the typewriter for a while (preferably doing something non-cerebral); then return when your mind has had time to rest and debug itself.

This trick works, but only if you fully comply. No halfhearted pauses, please. No two-minute trips to the refrigerator, no five-minute phone conversations. Diversion means, well, diversion. Go outside and walk at least several blocks or several miles. Watch TV for an hour or two. Go shopping. Take a swim, visit a friend, see a movie, have a nap, knit a sweater, play a round of Ping-Pong, read a mystery novel, build some shelves, cook a gourmet meal. The point is, change your impressions *entirely,* then, after one or preferably two hours, go back to work. By now your mind will present new materials uncoaxed. All it needed was time to recharge.

2. Relaxation Stop pushing against writer's block and try an easier way around: relax.

There are, of course, innumerable ways to go about this, from afternoon naps to neuro-linguistic programming. Some writers sit comfortably and listen to good music until their bodies feel refreshed. Some walk, trying to blank their mind of extraneous thoughts. Others meditate or do breathing exercises or listen to relaxation tapes or practice tension-release relaxation systems (lie flat on the floor and alternately tighten and relax the muscles in your face, neck, shoulders, chest, arms, stomach, back, and legs). Innumerable books exist on the subject of relaxation, and most are filled with excellent techniques. Try them.

3. Physical activity For me this last remedy is the most effective. I try not to let a day go by without getting in at least some physical exertion. It chases away cobwebs, gets blood flowing, and has a corresponding effect on my creative energies.

What exercise is best? It depends on your tastes. Check

with your doctor first, of course, then jog, play a sport, take a yoga class, do aerobics, calisthenics, martial arts, rapid walking, gymnastics, dance, weight lifting, tennis, fencing, swimming, whatever turns you on. The body and the mind are inextricably linked: What helps one will help the other.

Other temporary but nonetheless effective aids to unblocking the inventive mind include:

- Taking a shower.
- Drinking a cup of tea or coffee.
- Splashing cold water on your face, ears, and neck; placing a cold washcloth on top of your head.
- Taking a ten-minute walk.
- Opening the encyclopedia to any page and reading.
- Browsing in a store.
- Listening to a book on tape.
- Doing a few minutes of physical work around the house or apartment.
- Standing by a window and breathing deeply.
- Working at a hobby project.
- Reading the work of a favorite writer for ten minutes, returning to your writing with his or her words fresh in your mind.
- Standing, stretching, touching your toes, reaching for the ceiling, rotating your head and neck, and (health permitting) jogging in place.

Then go back to work.

Reward yourself.

For what? For the number of pages you have written in a day. For crafting a prose passage of quality and order. For working four straight hours without a break. For sticking to it though you yearned to do something else. Whatever. Set yourself a goal, determine what the reward will be, then fulfill it when you succeed.

With what? A cup of coffee at 11 o'clock for rereading a chapter twice. A nap after lunch for working all morning. A walk in the woods or through the park for compiling a tiresome bibliography. A candy bar for sitting in the library three hours straight doing research. A telephone call to a friend for writing a necessary letter. Really, it doesn't much matter what the bonus is as long as it gives you something to look forward to and to work toward. As every educator knows, people perform better when they know ahead of time that they will receive compensation for their efforts.

Keep a writer's log or journal.

Famous writers such as Kafka, Camus, Fitzgerald, Woolf, Trollope, Dostoevsky, Thoreau, and many others have done some of their finest literary work in journals and diaries. The very personal quality of the journal form, coupled with the absence of outside judgment and the lack of stylistic constraints, frees writers to produce literary forms that might otherwise never be attempted—or even dared.

The double blessing of a journal is that while you are keeping a record of daily events that will remain personally relevant for years to come, you are also practicing your art. In this way, like the child who becomes strong by lifting a calf every day until the calf grows into a steer, your writing style matures in tiny increments.

Write a little each day.

Whether it be a journal, a novel, a poem, a letter, just write. Write, write, write. Practice is your greatest teacher. Try your hand at a variety of different challenges. Ad copy. Diaries. Newspaper articles. Captions. One-liners. Articles. Letters. Editorials. Jokes. Testimonials. Reports. Summaries. Essays. Instructions. Memos. Epitaphs. *Anything* that keeps your pen fresh and your mind coining ideas. "It takes ten years to get to become a writer," Jules Renard once said, "and twenty years to become a good one." Every day counts.

Chapter
7

EXERCISES THAT BUILD WRITING SKILLS

A N excellent technique for enhancing literary skill is to spend five or ten minutes every day working on writing exercises. While these come in innumerable forms and formats, the following ones are, I believe, especially valuable for improving a writer's control over descriptive and emotive passages. If possible, try practicing one or two of these exercises regularly, every day if you can. The results will quickly show up in your work.

Describe an object by its parts and dimensions, without first telling the reader its name.

For instance: I have in front of me a rectangular piece of wood, six feet long by three feet wide by two inches thick. It is supported from the bottom by four, three-foot high, uniformly turned cylindrical wooden posts, one of which is located at each corner. Viola: a table.

Or: I have here a hollow cylinder four inches high. It is made of porcelain clay with a C-shaped handle attached to it. Its surface is shiny, vitreous, and blue. It is used to hold liquids. Voila: a cup.

And so forth.

This exercise can become amazingly demanding when you attempt to depict the action of objects such as a scissors or a folding chair. So start with easy items and work your way up. Then test the accuracy of your descriptions by reading them to others. See how long it takes them to recognize the object you are writing about.

Write a conversation between two people on any dramatic or intriguing subject.

Set the scene. Anything goes. For instance:

> Suppose one of your characters has just discovered that his wife is pregnant—with another man's child.
>
> Suppose a mother is talking to her son on the night before he goes off to war.
>
> Suppose two retarded persons are talking about God.
>
> Suppose a student meets the principal of his school perusing books in a pornographic bookstore.
>
> Suppose someone has just seen a metal statue come alive and is trying to make a friend believe it.
>
> Suppose Napoleon and Hitler are meeting in some mythical place, discussing their views on life and love.

Let the conversation run as long as its energy and interest endures. Don't throw it away when you are finished. Place it in your files (or notebook) and keep it. It's amazing how often excerpts from exercises like these end up getting used in actual writing projects.

Write a set of directions for a complicated task.

As most writers have discovered, phrasing directions in a clear, simple manner is one of the most challenging and tiring kinds of writing. It is *far* easier to tell readers about John's burning passion for Suzie or about the terrible volcano spewing lava over the helpless villagers than it is to explain how to construct a towel rack or how to adjust a bicycle seat.

Thus, if you want to really push your writing skills, try writing some simple directions. For example:

> Explain to a blind person how to crochet a sweater.
> Explain to a child how to frame a picture.
> Describe to a Martian how human beings wash their hands.

An interesting variation: As you've no doubt noticed, most instructions that accompany commercial do-it-yourself projects are badly written. Next time such a disaster comes your way, take these directions and rewrite them entirely, attempting with all your writer's skill to improve on them until they become an unmistakably clear piece of documentation.

Take a subject and write about it three different ways.

Again, it's not important what subject you choose. Start with a conversation. Or a description of a historical event, a speech, commercial instructions, a philosophical idea. Write it out clearly, reread it, correct it, and set it aside. Now write it a second time from a different perspective: different voice, different slant. Reread and put away. Then repeat a third time, trying again to approach the matter in yet a different way.

This one will stretch you to your limits, but it will cause your writing skills to grow by leaps and bounds. It will also demonstrate that it sometimes takes more than one effort to achieve the best expression of an idea. Charlie Chaplin, we are told, sometimes shot more than 100 takes of a scene before he allowed one to be printed. Flaubert would rewrite a short, one-page scene ten or twelve times before he was satisfied. Here's Hemingway on the reason he rewrote the last scene in *A Farewell to Arms* thirty-nine times: "Because I wanted to get the words right." "Genius," Einstein once remarked, "is the infinite capacity for taking pains." Practice this exercise —it's an exercise in taking pains.

Chapter

8

TIPS ON WRITING FROM FAMOUS WRITERS

ALL writers, especially the great ones, develop devices, shortcuts, stratagems, and expedients which help them work with increased clarity and confidence. Many of them have been willing to share their secrets, though sometimes they reveal them in oblique and even cryptic ways.

What follows is a selection of statements on a variety of stylistic subjects culled from the greats and semigreats of literature. Most are direct and straightforward, though in a few the inner wisdom is concealed from direct view. All are worthy of consideration. (You might, by the way, try adding quotes and aphorisms from your own favorite writers to this list. Salient advice from the greats is a terrific subject for any writer's notebook.)

"This is what Meander replied when, as the day approached for which he had promised a comedy, and he was reproved for not having yet set his hand to the task: 'It is put together and ready; the only thing left to do is to add the verses to it.' "

—MONTAIGNE

"I don't think characters turn out the way you think they are going to turn out. They don't always go your way. If I wanted to start writing about you, by page ten I probably wouldn't be. I don't think you start with a person. I think you start with the parts of many people. Drama has to do with conflict in people, with denials."

—LILLIAN HELLMAN

"Men do not understand books until they have had a certain amount of life. Or at any rate, no man understands a deep book until he has seen and lived at least part of its contents."

—EZRA POUND

"If you would be pungent, be brief; for it is as with words as with sunbeams. The more they are condensed, the deeper they burn."

—ROBERT SOUTHEY

"Whatever we conceive well we express clearly."

—BOILEAU

"I don't know how to please your readers. Those're people with whom you've got to be gentle. . . . You can't beat them up. They like us to amuse them without abusing them."

—LOUIS-FERDINAND CELINE

"The aim of art is to represent not the outward appearance of things, but their inward significance; for this, and not the external mannerism and detail, is true reality."

—ARISTOTLE

"Read, read, read. Read everything—trash, classics, good and bad, and see how they do it. Just like a carpenter who works as an apprentice and studies the master. Read! You'll absorb it. Then write. If it is good, you'll find out. If it's not, throw it out the window."

—WILLIAM FAULKNER

"A writer is someone who can make a riddle out of an answer."

—KARL KRAUS

"It's not so much what you say in a book that constitutes its value . . . (but) all you would like to say, which nourishes it secretly."

—ANDRE GIDE

"How, then, does the beginning writer recognize a good idea when it comes to him? First of all by its originality; second by the excitement it engenders in him to get to a typewriter; third by its ability to attract good characters, to collect places where the idea must happen, to end somewhere, to put characters under stress, to force characters to act, and finally to resolve itself."

—JAMES GUN

121

"What makes a good writer of history is a guy who is suspicious. Suspicion marks the real difference between the man who wants to write honest history and the ones who'd rather write a good story."

—JIM BISHOP

"I just think it's bad to talk about one's present work, for it spoils something at the root of the creative act. It discharges the tension."

—NORMAN MAILER

"It is a great fault, in descriptive poetry, to describe everything."

—ALEXANDER POPE

"To the mind of . . . a writer, clearness in the narrow sense—the thin lucidity of what passes at times for scientific statement—is not enough. He seeks to raise mere logical precision to higher powers of veracity by mobilizing the subtler evocative values of words, their richness in secondary suggestions, their capacity to stimulate in the reader intuitive faculties more penetrative than formal reasoning."

—C. E. MONTAGUE

"If you have anything to say, anything you feel nobody has ever said before, you have got to feel it so desperately that you will find some way to say it that nobody has ever found before, so that the thing you have to say and the way of saying it blend as one matter—as indissolubly as if they were conceived together.

—F. SCOTT FITZGERALD

. . . [the] care for shimmering set, active plot, bright characters, change of pace and gaiety should *all show in the plan*. Leave *out* one or two, and your novel is weaker, three or four and you're running a department store with only half the counters open."

—F. SCOTT FITZGERALD

"When you think of something abstract you are more inclined to use words from the start, and unless you make a conscious effort to prevent it, the existing dialect will come rushing in and do the job for you, at the expense of blurring or even changing your meaning. Probably it is better to put off using words as long as possible and get one's meaning as clear as one can through pictures or sensations. Afterwards one can choose—not simply *accept*—the phrases that will best cover the meaning, and then switch round and decide what impression one's words are likely to make on another person. This last effort of the mind cuts out all stale or mixed images, all prefabricated phrases, needless repetitions, and humbug and vagueness generally."

—GEORGE ORWELL

"It would be endless to run over the several defects of style among us: I shall therefore say nothing of the *mean* and the *paultry,* much less of the *slovenly* and *indecent.*

Two things I will just warn you against: the first is, the frequency of flat, unnecessary epithets; and the other is, the folly of using old threadbare phrases which . . . are nauseous to rational hearers, and will seldom express your meaning as well as your own natural words."

—JONATHAN SWIFT

"The strength and balance of his [Swift's] sentences are due to an exquisite taste. As I had done before I copied passages and then tried to write them out again from memory. I tried altering words or the order in which they were set. I found that the only possible words were those Swift had used and that the order in which he had placed them was the only possible order."

—W. SOMERSET MAUGHAM

"No matter how good a phrase or a simile he may have, if he puts it in where it is not absolutely necessary and irreplaceable he is spoiling his work for egotism."

—ERNEST HEMINGWAY

"My purpose in writing is to entertain myself first and other people secondly."

—JOHN MACDONALD

"Any writer overwhelmingly honest about pleasing himself is almost sure to please others."

—MARIANNE MOORE

—"A sentence should read as if its author, had he held a plow instead of a pen, could have drawn a furrow deep and straight to the end."

—HENRY DAVID THOREAU

Sir, you may have remarked, that the making of a partial change, without a due regard to the general structure of a sentence, is a very frequent cause of error in a composition.

—SAMUEL JOHNSON

"Too much ornament is a fault in every kind of production. Uncommon expressions, strong flashes of wit, pointed similes, and epigrammatic turns, especially when they recur too frequently, are a disfigurement, rather than any embellishment of discourse. . . . the mind, in perusing a work overstocked with wit, is fatigued and disgusted with the constant endeavor to shine and suprise. This is the case where a writer overabounds in wit, even though that wit, in itself, should be just and agreeable. But it commonly happens to such writers, that they seek for their favorite ornaments, even where the subject does not afford them; and by that means have twenty insipid conceits for one thought which is really beautiful."

—DAVID HUME

"Fine writing, according to Mr. Addison, consists of sentiments, which are natural, without being obvious. There cannot be a juster, and more concise definition of fine writing."

—DAVID HUME

"You cannot write by thinking. You have plenty of time to think in between times. The period in between is when you *stuff* your eyeballs, when you read diversified multitudes of material in every field. I absolutely demand of you and everyone I know that they be widely read in every damn field there is: in every religion and every art form and *don't* tell me you haven't got time! There's plenty of time. You need all of these cross-references. You never know when your head is going to use this fuel, this food for its purposes."

—RAY BRADBURY

"I've never written for money. I've written just because of an imbecilic urge."

—CHARLES BUKOWSKI

Suggested Readings

Egri, Lagos, *The Art of Dramatic Writing*. New York: Simon and Schuster, 1960.

Eisenberg, Anne, *Effective Technical Communication*. New York: McGraw Hill, 1982.

Hall, Donald, *Writing Well*. Boston: Little, Brown, 1985.

Lanham, Richard, *Revising Prose*. New York: Charles Scribner's Sons, 1979.

Murry, Donald, *Write to Learn*. New York: Holt, Rinehart and Winston, 1984.

Strunk, William and White, E.B., *The Elements of Style*. New York: Macmillan, n.d. (third edition).

Suggested Readings